MW01048009

Inn the Keeper's Kitchen ™

A Collection of Recipe Secrets
from Award-Winning Bed & Breakfasts and Country Inns

From the Publishers of Inn Traveler® and Bed & Breakfast Journal®

Arrington Publishing

214 W. Texas, Suite 400 • Midland, Texas 79701
(432) 684-6800 • www.bnbjournal.com
e-mail: info@bnbjournal.com

© 2005 by Arrington Publishing
214 W. Texas, Suite 400
Midland, Texas 79701
(432) 684-6800
www.bnbjournal.com

Inn the Keeper's Kitchen™, *Arrington's Inn Traveler®*, and *Arrington's Bed & Breakfast Journal®*
are federally registered trademarks of Arrington Publishing.

All rights reserved. No part of this publication may be reproduced in any form or by any means,
electronic or mechanical, including photocopy and information storage and retrieval system,
without permission in writing from Arrington Publishing.

The recipes contained in this book are to be followed exactly as written. Neither the publisher
nor the author(s) are responsible for any specific health or allergy needs that may require medical
supervision, or for any adverse reactions to the recipes contained in this book.

The information in this book was supplied in large part by the inns themselves and is subject
to change without notice. The publisher makes no representation that this book is accurate or
complete. Errors and omissions, whether typographical, clerical or otherwise,
may sometimes occur herein.

ISBN: 0-9769783-1-8

Publisher
David H. Arrington

Cookbook Coordinator/Editor
Tiffany Fowlkes

Managing Editor
Pattie Hoover

Assistant Editor
Sarah Stiles

Production Manager
Tonia Ingram

Cover photography by:
Jean Becq of Becq Photography International, Calgary

Printed and manufactured by:

Quebecor World Eusey Press
27 Nashua Street
Leominster, MA 01453

First printing: 2005 - 5,000 copies

Inn the Keeper's Kitchen™

Arrington Publishing
214 W. Texas, Suite 400
Midland, Texas 79701
Telephone: (432) 684-6800   Fax: (432) 684-5374
E-mail: info@bnbjournal.com
Visit our Web site at www.bnbjournal.com

Name _

Address _

City _ State _ _ _ _ _ _ Zip _ _ _ _ _ _ _ _

Please send _____ copies at $15.95 each   _ _ _ _ _ _ _
Texas residents add sales tax $1.32 each   _ _ _ _ _ _ _ _
Postage and handling $5.00 each   _ _ _ _ _ _ _
Total   _ _ _ _ _ _ _ _ _ _

Make checks payable to *Arrington Publishing*

Card number: _ Expiration date: _ _ _ _ _ _ _

Signature: _

Canadian residents, please contact Arrington Publishing for shipping charges.

✂ -

Inn the Keeper's Kitchen™

Arrington Publishing
214 W. Texas, Suite 400
Midland, Texas 79701
Telephone: (432) 684-6800   Fax: (432) 684-5374
E-mail: info@bnbjournal.com
Visit our Web site at www.bnbjournal.com

Name _

Address _

City _ State _ _ _ _ _ _ Zip _ _ _ _ _ _ _ _

Please send _____ copies at $15.95 each   _ _ _ _ _ _ _
Texas residents add sales tax $1.32 each   _ _ _ _ _ _ _ _
Postage and handling $5.00 each   _ _ _ _ _ _ _
Total   _ _ _ _ _ _ _ _ _ _

Make checks payable to *Arrington Publishing*

Card number: _ Expiration date: _ _ _ _ _ _ _

Signature: _

Canadian residents, please contact Arrington Publishing for shipping charges.

Introduction

Arrington Publishing is pleased to present this exciting collection of signature bed & breakfast and country inn recipes. We are confident that you will be delighted to add this distinctive series to your recipe and cookbook collection.

The recipes featured in this cookbook are unique in that they are signature recipes from innkeepers located throughout North America. The most notable aspect about the recipes is that they are bed & breakfast and country inn cuisine category winners from our annual *Book of Lists* awards. Each year, Arrington Publishing hosts a contest in which inngoers vote for their favorite bed & breakfast and country inn in various categories such as "Best Breakfast in the USA." There are over 35 categories, and each category winner represents the top 3 percent of the finest establishments in the United States and Canada.

When we started this cookbook project, we had many ideas for presenting our special innkeeper recipes and realized that our most recent cuisine category *Book of Lists* award winners should be in the spotlight. After all, they were voted as having the best food by their guests!

There are many great features included in this cookbook. Not only will you be able to reproduce the exquisite dishes, but you will be enlightened by the tips and hints included with the recipes. Did you know that George Washington had a personal recipe for eggnog or that Thomas Jefferson was a big fan of hot chocolate? Did you know that when poaching eggs you will get the best results with fresh eggs? Throughout the entire cookbook we have included helpful hints and "did you know" tips and tidbits such as these for your cooking enjoyment. And, just in case you might have forgotten just how much a "dash" equals, we have included a measuring guide for all your measuring questions. On page 163, you will find our detailed index listing more than 100 dishes by title, category and/or main ingredient. On page 167, is an index listing over 40 bed & breakfasts and country inns that are featured in the cookbook, along with contact information and the *Book of Lists* category in which they won.

You might want to take the afternoon to sit down in a comfy resting place with a hot cup of coffee or tea and peruse through our cookbook. As you look through the pages, we hope that you will be inspired to recreate the warmth, comfort and love that each innkeeper instills within each recipe they share with their guests. We have included a "Personal Touches" area for you to make notes and adjustments or to note how much you enjoyed the dish when you made it. We hope you enjoy our cookbook as much as we have enjoyed preparing it for you! May your kitchen be full of warmth, joy and happiness!

Warm regards,
The staff of Arrington Publishing

Table of Contents

Breakfast Entrées

Breads

Cocktails & Beginnings

Dinner Entrées

Sweet Endings

Dear Readers,

Think about the last time you actually prepared a meal in your kitchen. Was it yesterday, last week, last month? Did you enjoy the ceremony of preparing nourishment for your loved ones, or was it a process of dread and despair? It seems our practice of preparing home cooked meals is fast becoming the lesser-desired option to the instant satisfaction of fast food and restaurants.

Breaking bread with another has been a significant event among humans for centuries. Cookbooks, recipes, preparing food and sharing it with loved ones are a significant aspect of each and every one of our lives. I'll bet you can recall several pleasing memories that involve cooking or enjoying a meal with your family and friends.

My wife, Shelley, and I received this pancake recipe more than 10 years ago from our dear friend Marian Nichols, and it has been a Saturday morning family tradition ever since. My children are as much a part of the process as Shelley and I. Their favorite part of preparing the pancakes is flipping them on the griddle. Don't forget the yummy toppings. Ellen loves to add strawberries to her pancakes, while Katie Grace really likes chocolate chips. Amy enjoys hers topped with powdered sugar, and D.J. just likes to eat as many as he can. I prefer them plain, and as my children say, "They are the best pancakes in the world."

I would like to share this recipe with you and your loved ones, and I hope you will enjoy it as much as we have. Maybe you will find this recipe, or one of the award-winning recipes in the following pages, great for a Saturday morning tradition with your family. From my family to yours, happy cooking!

Sincerely,

David H. Arrington

Marian's French Pancakes

"A favorite of David Arrington and family"

1/2 cup flour
1 teaspoon baking powder
1/4 teaspoon salt
1 egg
1 cup hot milk
2 tablespoons melted butter

Sift together flour, baking powder and salt. Set aside. In a separate bowl, beat egg lightly. Add hot milk and melted butter. Stir into dry ingredients, and beat until perfectly smooth. Makes a very thin batter. Heat griddle to about 350 degrees, and grease with a small amount of cooking oil. Make crepe-like pancakes approximately 3 inches in diameter.

On the Cover...

Cheddar and Chive Soufflé

1 teaspoon garlic, minced
2 cups dry white wine
4-1/2 tablespoons butter
1/3 cup all-purpose flour
1 cup milk
1-3/4 cups old Cheddar, grated
Salt and white pepper, to taste
5 eggs, separated
1/3 cup fresh chives, sliced

photography by: Jean Becq of Becq Photography International, Calgary

Melt 1 teaspoon butter in a small saucepan. Add garlic and sauté over medium high heat for 1 or 2 minutes. Add white wine. Simmer mixture over medium high heat to reduce the volume by 3/4; about 1/2 cup liquid should be left in the pan. In a separate bowl, stir the remaining butter and flour into a smooth paste. Add the paste to the wine reduction and whisk well. Cook over medium high heat until the mixture bubbles and thickens, about 3 to 5 minutes. Add 1/2 of the milk. Whisk well to eliminate any lumps.

Add the remaining milk and whisk well. Bring the mixture to a boil. The mixture should become quite thick. Turn off the heat or remove pan from the stove. Add 1 cup cheese and stir gently. Season to taste with salt and pepper.

Preheat oven to 400 degrees and position the rack in center. Lightly butter 4 – 8-ounce ramekins and have them ready on a cookie sheet. Put egg whites in a clean glass, ceramic or stainless steel bowl. Whisk to a soft, almost firm peek but avoid over whisking into dry clumps.

In a separate bowl, stir egg yolks with 1/2 cup warm cheese sauce. Add remaining sauce, cheese and chives. Stir well. Fold in egg whites with a large rubber spatula; avoid over folding.

Divide mixture among ramekins on the baking sheet and place them in the oven. Bake 15 to 20 minutes. Avoid peeking. The soufflé is done when it is puffed up and golden; the outer edges should be firm to the touch, but the center should still be soft and jiggle when you gently shake the tray. Serve immediately.

Servings: 4

Presented by: Kensington Riverside Inn - Calgary, Alberta

Breakfast
Entrées

egg variations

Cornish Baked Eggs

1 tablespoon butter
1/2 English muffin, 1 slice bread or 1/2 biscuit
1/4 cup Parmesan cheese, grated
1 egg, separated
1 teaspoon parsley, chives, thyme
   or other savory herbs, chopped
Salt to taste
Pepper to taste

Preheat oven to 375 degrees. Butter English muffin or choice of bread and sprinkle with Parmesan cheese. Place on baking sheet and set aside. Beat egg white until stiff but not dry. Fold in herbs. Mound the egg white on the split prepared English muffin or bread choice. Gently push the yolk into the middle of the egg white; push it down to hold in place. Sprinkle liberally with Parmesan cheese, and lightly salt and pepper. Bake for 8 to 12 minutes. Serve immediately.

Servings: 1 per person

Presented by: Inn Britannia - Searsport, Maine

Personal touches . . .

_____

_____

_____

_____

_____

_____

_____

Did you know . . . eggs are a perishable food and should be refrigerated. Keep eggs in their original carton and in the coldest part of your refrigerator for up to 5 weeks. Throw away any eggs that are cracked, broken or leaking.

Dilled Crab Scramble for Two

1 tablespoon butter
5 eggs
2 tablespoons ranch dressing
1 – 6-ounce can crab meat, drained
Dash of lemon-pepper to taste
Dash of chopped fresh dill to taste
2 ounces cream cheese, cubed
2 tablespoons Cheddar cheese, shredded
Sprinkle of blended cheeses (Mexican works well)

Garnish:
Fresh dill sprigs

Melt butter in skillet. Beat eggs, ranch dressing, crab and seasonings. Cook in skillet until almost set, stirring frequently. Stir in cream cheese and Cheddar cheese. Cook 1 to 2 minutes, or until eggs are set. Divide into 2 servings and sprinkle with shredded cheese. Garnish with fresh dill sprig.

Servings: 2

Presented by: Celebrations Inn, a Festive Bed & Breakfast - Pomfret Center, Connecticut

Personal touches . . .

_____

_____

_____

_____

_____

_____

_____

Breakfast Rellenos

2 Anaheim or Poblano chilies
1 tablespoon piñon nuts, raw
2 eggs
1 tablespoon golden raisins
4 tablespoons sour cream
1/2 cup Farmer's cheese, grated

Garnish:
Avocado, sliced

Align chilies on a foil-covered cookie sheet. Place 4 to 6 inches below the broiler unit. Roast chilies for 6 to 8 minutes, rotating occasionally, until lightly charred and uniformly blistered. Remove from the broiler, and place in a plastic bag; close tightly. Steam for 5 minutes. Remove from bag, and wash under cold water to remove the skin, making sure to leave stems in place. Make a slit lengthwise in the chili and remove the seeds. Pat dry with a paper towel and place on an oven-proof plate, slit side up. Roast piñon nuts in a small iron skillet over low heat until brown. Stir often to prevent scorching. Scramble the eggs with piñon nuts and raisins. Spoon the egg mixture into the prepared chilies. Spoon sour cream over eggs, and sprinkle cheese on top. Place under the broiler until cheese melts. Place on serving dish and garnish with avocado slices.

Servings: 1 per person

Presented by: Hughes Hacienda Bed & Breakfast - Colorado Springs, Colorado

helpful hints . . .

The Spanish term for pine nuts is pignolias or piñon. Piñons have a sweet, faint pine flavor. They will turn rancid quickly and should be stored in an airtight container in the refrigerator for up to two months, or up to six months in the freezer.

Personal touches . . .

_____

_____

_____

_____

_____

_____

*Did you know . . .
it is a good idea to
wear rubber gloves
when working with
peppers because oil
can get on hands and
squirt everywhere.
Do not wipe your
face with the back of
your hand, as the
spray can travel up
to one foot. After
handling, rub your
hands with lemon
juice and wash your
hands several times
in warm, soapy
water.*

Silverton Eggs Supreme

6 – 8-inch or 10-inch unrefrigerated flour tortillas,
   homemade if possible
6 ounces sharp Cheddar cheese, shredded
3 medium roasted green chilies, diced
1 small onion, chopped
1 medium tomato, chopped
2 sprigs fresh basil, leaves finely chopped
9 large eggs
1 teaspoon Coleman's dry mustard
1/2 teaspoon garlic powder
1/2 teaspoon fresh ground black pepper
1/2 teaspoon salt

Preheat oven to 375 degrees. Using a jumbo muffin pan,
fold tortillas to fit each muffin cup (somewhat like a cone
with a flat tip). Place 1/2 of the cheese in each tortilla
cone. Distribute chilies, onion, tomato and basil evenly
into each cone. In a separate bowl, beat eggs; add dry
mustard, garlic powder, pepper and salt. Pour egg mixture
evenly into each cone. Distribute remaining cheese on top
of egg mixture. Bake in the middle of oven 40 to 50 minutes until edges of tortillas are golden brown and cheese is
light brown.

*This entrée has a habit of rolling around on the plate – an
orange wedge on one side and a nice arrangement of tarragon roasted potatoes on the other side will keep it from
rolling around. To enhance presentation, place a small
dollop of sour cream close to the entrée, sprinkle a small
amount of paprika on top of the sour cream and stick a
small basil leaf in the sour cream. If the basil leaves are
wilted, soak them in ice water for a few minutes and pat
dry. Finalize the presentation by placing a few 1/2 tea-
spoon-sized dollops of medium picante sauce or salsa
evenly around the rim of the plate, and sprinkle the top of
the dish with a few chopped chives.*

**Personal
touches . . .**

Servings: 6

Presented by: The Wyman Hotel & Inn - Silverton, Colorado

Paradise Egg Dish

6 to 8 slices bacon
8 to 10 eggs
1 cup milk
1/2 cup green chilies, chopped
1 cup cottage cheese
3/4 cup sour cream
2 cups cheese (any type), shredded or sliced

Preheat oven to 325 degrees. Grease an 8 x 12 baking dish. Cook bacon strips. Drain, crumble and set aside. Mix eggs and milk; pour into heated skillet along with at least 1 tablespoon of bacon grease. Scramble lightly. Stir in green chilies and cottage cheese. Spoon into greased baking dish. Spread sour cream over mixture. Sprinkle bacon bits on top of sour cream. Cover with cheese. Bake for 20 to 30 minutes until ingredients are heated through and cheese is melted.

Servings: 4

Presented by: Pikes Peak Paradise Bed and Breakfast - Woodland Park, Colorado

Personal touches . . .

_____
_____
_____
_____
_____
_____
_____

Did you know . . . cottage cheese is available in three forms: small-curd, medium-curd and large-curd. Cartons of cottage cheese are stamped on the bottom with the date they should be pulled from the shelves because it is more perishable than other cheeses. Cottage cheese should be stored in the coldest part of the refrigerator and is good for up to 10 days past the stamped date.

Personal touches . . .

Baked Eggs with Three Cheeses

4 eggs
1-1/2 cups milk
1 teaspoon sugar
2 cups cheese, shredded
   (preferably a Mexican four cheese blend)
2 ounces cream cheese, cubed
1 cup small curd cottage cheese
1/3 cup butter, melted
4 ounces green chilies, diced
1/4 cup flour (1 tablespoon cornstarch can be substituted)
1/2 teaspoon baking powder

Preheat oven to 350 degrees and spray a 1-1/2 quart baking dish with non-stick cooking spray. Beat together eggs, milk and sugar. Add cheeses, melted butter and chilies. Mix well. Mix in flour and baking powder and pour into baking dish. Bake 45 to 50 minutes or until knife inserted in center comes out clean.

May be prepared in advance and refrigerated, covered. Uncover and bake up to 60 minutes.

Servings: 4 to 6

Presented by: Desert Willow Bed & Breakfast - Jemez Springs, New Mexico

Gold Rush Baked Eggs & Cheese

7 eggs
1 cup milk
1-3/4 teaspoons sugar
1 pound cheese (combination of any type), grated
5 ounces cream cheese, room temperature and cubed
1 – 16-ounce container small curd cottage cheese
5 tablespoons butter, room temperature and cubed
1/2 cup flour
1 teaspoon baking powder

Preheat oven to 350 degrees and spray a 9 x 13 glass baking dish with non-stick cooking spray. Beat eggs, milk and sugar until combined. Add all of the cheeses and butter, and mix well. Add flour and baking powder, and mix well. Pour into baking dish, and bake for 45 minutes or until knife inserted into middle comes out clean.

May be prepared a day ahead and refrigerated overnight, but baking time will increase to about an hour. Any combination of meats and vegetables may be added for variety. Suggested combinations: ham, bacon, mushrooms, green peppers and/or squash.

Presented by: Alaska Gold Rush Bed & Breakfast Inn - Palmer, Alaska

Personal touches . . .

_____

_____

_____

_____

_____

_____

_____

Mexican Eggs

1 can mild enchilada sauce
2 corn tortillas per serving
1 can low fat refried black beans
2 strips bacon per serving
1/2 cup Cheddar, Monterey Jack or
    Mexican cheese mix, shredded
2 eggs per serving
1 tomato, chopped
1 dollop sour cream per serving

Garnish:
Sliced olives

Preheat oven to 325 degrees. Preheat enchilada sauce. Place 2 corn tortillas on each plate. Warm refried black beans with a small amount of water in a saucepan. Spread 2 to 3 tablespoons of beans in the center of each tortilla. Place two strips of crisped bacon alongside the beans on the edges of the tortillas. Top with a generous sprinkling of shredded cheese. Place plates with prepared tortillas in oven to melt cheese for about 10 minutes as you prepare the eggs.

Immediately poach eggs in preheated enchilada sauce approximately 4-1/2 minutes or until cooked to your preference. Place poached eggs on top of prepared tortillas. Top with enchilada sauce, cheese, chopped tomatoes and a dollop of sour cream. Garnish with sliced olives.

Personal touches . . .

Adjust the spiciness of the dish by increasing the heat of the enchilada sauce from mild to medium or hot. Do not allow the tortillas to dry out in the oven; warm them through enough to melt the cheese.

Servings: 1 per person

Presented by: Casa de San Pedro Bed & Breakfast Inn - Hereford, Arizona

helpful hints . . .

Fresh eggs are the best for poaching. When eggs are more than a week old, the whites thin out and gather compactly around the yolk, making a rounder, neater shape. Use eggs right out of the refrigerator.

Did you know . . . masa is the Spanish word for "dough." It is the traditional dough used for making corn tortillas. It's made with sun- or fire-dried corn kernels that have been cooked in limewater. After the kernels have been cooked, they are soaked in the limewater overnight and the wet corn is ground into masa.

Personal touches . . .

_____

_____

_____

_____

_____

_____

Earle Clarke House Strip Tease Eggs...with Tassels

There's nothing resembling a tassel anywhere in this dish. One of our favorite guests, a mystery writer, christened it "Strip Tease Eggs with Tassels," and that is how it remained to be called. He's the head of psychiatry for a big hospital, so analyze that!

4 slices bacon
8 pieces focaccia, sourdough or French bread,
    thickly sliced
4 teaspoons cream cheese
4 teaspoons Asiago cheese, shredded
1 package chopped frozen spinach
1/2 cup homemade beef stock, chicken stock
    or water and a bouillon cube
1 tablespoon butter
1/4 teaspoon fresh nutmeg, grated
8 eggs

Prepare the topping: Fry the slices of bacon until crisp. Drain on paper towel, crumble and set aside. If you're serving vegetarians, toasted sunflower seeds make a good substitution.

Prepare the toast: Generously spread each slice of bread with cream cheese, then sprinkle liberally with shredded cheese. Place on a baking sheet and set aside while you prepare the spinach and eggs.

Preheat your oven broiler.

Prepare the spinach: Poach spinach in a small amount of stock or bouillon. Drain well in a sieve. Add butter and nutmeg to drained spinach, and set aside in a warm place.

Personal touches . . .

_____

_____

_____

_____

_____

_____

Poach the eggs: Use range-free eggs, if possible. One minute before they are ready, run the toast rounds under the broiler until slightly browned.

Assemble your masterpiece: Put a small amount of spinach on each toast round, top with an egg and sprinkle with bacon or sunflower seeds. Serve with coarsely ground pepper.

Servings: 4

Presented by: Earle Clarke House - Victoria, British Columbia

Did you know...
the Italian bread
Focaccia begins as a
large, flat round that
is liberally brushed
or drizzled with olive
oil and sprinkled
with salt. Slightly
sour with a tangy
flavor, sourdough
bread is created by
using a special yeast
starter as the
leavener. Most
sourdoughs are made
from all-purpose
flour. However,
there are many
delicious variations
including those made
from whole-wheat or
rye flour. French
bread is a light,
crusty, yeast-raised
bread that is made
with water instead of
milk.

Personal
touches . . .

_____

_____

_____

_____

_____

_____

_____

Did you know . . . spinach originated in the Middle East and was grown in Spain during the 8th century. The Spaniards are the ones who eventually brought it to the United States. Fresh spinach is available year-round. When choosing spinach, select leaves that are crisp and dark green with a nice fresh fragrance. Avoid leaves that are limp, damaged or that have yellow spots. Spinach can be refrigerated in a plastic bag for up to 3 days. Usually very gritty, it must be thoroughly rinsed.

Personal touches . . .

Ham & Eggs at the Inn

2 tablespoons unsalted butter
3/4 pound mushrooms, finely chopped
1/4 cup shallots, finely chopped
1 bag fresh baby spinach, coarsely chopped
1/2 teaspoon salt
1/4 teaspoon black pepper
1 tablespoon fresh tarragon, finely chopped
1 tablespoon chives, minced
1/2 cup Swiss cheese, shredded
1/2 cup Gruyere cheese, shredded
12 slices Virginia ham (about 10 ounces)
12 medium eggs

Preheat oven to 400 degrees. Melt butter in skillet. Sauté mushrooms and shallots until tender, about 10 minutes. Drain off any liquid from the mushrooms. Add spinach, salt, pepper, tarragon and chives. Remove from heat after spinach is wilted, which will just take a minute or two. Stir in the cheeses. Using a 12-cup muffin pan, fit one slice of ham into each individual cup. Edges will stick up. Divide vegetable and cheese mixture into each cup. Gently crack 1 egg into each cup. Loosely cover with foil. Bake about 15 minutes or until eggs are set.

Servings: 6

Presented by: Celebrations Inn, a Festive Bed & Breakfast - Pomfret Center, Connecticut

A Rover's Soufflé

2 ounces cooked ham, chopped into small cubes
1/2 green onion, thinly chopped
1 medium white mushroom, thinly chopped
2 ounces of two different cheeses (1 ounce each),
  aged Cheddar and aged Gouda are recommended
1 large egg
1/4 cup milk
1/4 cup flour

Preheat oven to 325 degrees. Spray individual 12-ounce oven-safe ramekins with non-stick cooking spray. Wipe with paper towel to evenly coat bottom and sides. Layer cooked ham, green onion and mushroom in each ramekin. Grate the 2 cheeses and set aside. Using a cocktail blender, whip the egg, milk and flour on high to get as much air into the mixture as possible, about 30 seconds. Pour mixture evenly over ingredients in each ramekin. Sprinkle cheese combination over top, bake for 20 minutes and then broil for 5 minutes.

Servings: 12

Presented by: A Rover's Rest Bed and Breakfast - Blind Bay, British Columbia

Did you know . . . when using cutting boards, it is best to have one for meat, fish and poultry and one for foods that will be served raw. Discard cutting boards when they get excessively worn or hard-to-clean cracks appear. For effective cleaning, cutting boards should be washed with hot soapy water after each use.

Personal touches . . .

_____
_____
_____
_____
_____
_____
_____

Did you know . . .
Monterey Jack cheese was named such because it originated in Monterey, California. Monterey Jack is a versatile cheese and can be made from whole, partly skimmed or skimmed cow's milk. The high moisture and good melting properties make it excellent for sand-wiches as well as for cooked dishes.

Santa Fe Breakfast

8 large eggs
3/4 cup flour
2 teaspoons baking powder
1/2 teaspoon salt
1 teaspoon garlic, chopped
1 can whole corn (15 ounces)
1 can Ro*Tel® tomatoes & green chilies
12 ounces sour cream
1 pint cottage cheese, small-curd
3 cups Monterey Jack cheese, shredded

Garnish:
1 dollop sour cream per serving
Grape tomatoes

Preheat oven to 375 degrees and grease a 9 x 13 baking pan or dish. In a large bowl, beat eggs. Add flour, baking powder, salt, garlic, corn and Ro*Tel®, and mix well. Add sour cream and cottage cheese to the egg mixture, and blend well. Gently fold in Monterey Jack cheese, and stir until combined. Pour into pan and bake 50 to 60 minutes or until slightly brown. Serve with a dollop of sour cream and a grape tomato.

Servings: 8

Presented by: Wander Inn - Newport, Rhode Island

Personal touches . . .

_____

_____

_____

_____

_____

_____

_____

Godfather Eggs

1 cup red peppers, chopped and sautéed
1 bunch scallions, chopped and sautéed
8 eggs
1 cup Bisquick®
1 stick butter, melted
8 ounces cottage cheese
8 ounces ricotta cheese
8 ounces mozzarella cheese, shredded
1 cup milk
1 cup fresh basil
5 plum tomatoes, sliced

Preheat oven to 350 degrees, and generously spray a baking pan with non-stick cooking spray. Sauté red peppers and scallions, let cool. Lightly beat eggs, then mix all ingredients (except tomatoes) together. Pour into baking pan. Arrange tomatoes on top. Bake uncovered for 45 to 50 minutes until the edges just begin to brown.

The ingredients of this recipe will have you think the eggs are heavy, yet they are surprisingly light and absolutely delicious. Try serving them with sweet Italian sausage and crusty homemade Italian bread. Store bought baguettes are fine in a pinch!

Servings: 4 to 6

Presented by: The Evergreen Inn Bed & Breakfast - Spring Lake, New Jersey

Did you know . . . sweet, green bell peppers have twice as much vitamin C as oranges; red and yellow bell peppers have four times as much.

Personal touches . . .

Did you know . . .
when avocado flesh is cut and exposed to the air it tends to discolor rapidly. To minimize this effect it is always advisable to add avocado to a dish at the last moment.

Fiesta Olé

1 bag tater tots
Mrs. Dash® seasoning
2/3 cup real bacon bits and pieces
1 dozen eggs, scrambled
12 teaspoons sour cream
2 large tomatoes, diced
1 large can diced green chilies
1 bunch green onions, diced
2 to 3 cups Cheddar cheese, grated

Garnish:
Avocado, sliced
1 tomato, sliced (one slice per serving)
1 teaspoon salsa per serving
Parsley sprigs

Preheat oven to 400 degrees. Place tater tots in a 9 x 12 baking dish, sprinkle with Mrs. Dash® seasoning and bake for 15 minutes. When tater tots are completely cooked, smash with a potato masher to make a level "shell" within the baking dish. Sprinkle bacon bits over tater tot layer. Spread scrambled eggs over the top of the bacon bits. Place dollops of sour cream on top of eggs. Complete with layers of tomatoes, chilies, onions and cheese. Bake 20 minutes. Remove from oven and let stand for 5 minutes before cutting and serving. Garnish with a slice of avocado, slice of tomato, salsa and a sprig of parsley.

Personal touches . . .

Servings: 12

Presented by: The Roosevelt, a Bed and Breakfast Inn - Coeur d'Alene, Idaho

Sausage Pie a la Mode

3/4 cup sausage, diced*
3/4 cup Muenster cheese, diced*
1 cup milk
2 eggs
3/4 cup flour

* You can use various meat and cheese combinations for substitutions.

Preheat oven to 400 degrees and lightly butter a 9-inch pie plate. Mix all ingredients together until smooth. Pour into pie plate, and bake 30 to 35 minutes.

Servings: 4 to 6

Presented by: The Painted Lady Bed and Breakfast - Elmira, New York

Did you know . . .
Muenster was originally produced in France's Alsace region. European versions have red or orange rinds and a smooth, yellow interior with small holes. Its texture is semi-soft, and the flavor ranges from mild when young to quite assertive when aged. American versions have an orange rind, a lighter yellow interior and a decidedly bland flavor that in no way resembles the more robust European originals.

Personal touches . . .

_____
_____
_____
_____
_____
_____
_____

Did you know . . .
white pepper is a
less pungent
peppercorn that has
been allowed to
ripen, after which
the skin is removed
and the berry is
dried. This produces
the result of a
smaller, smoother-
skinned, light-tan
berry with a milder
flavor. White pepper
is most often used for
appearance. Usually
used for light-colored
sauces or foods
where dark specks of
black pepper would
stand out.

Breakfast Enchiladas

White Sauce:
2 tablespoons butter
2 tablespoons flour
1 cup chicken broth
Salt to taste
White pepper to taste
1 fresh, raw Serrano chili, finely chopped

Enchiladas:
1/4 cup corn oil
4 corn tortillas
6 large eggs
1/4 cup zucchini squash, diced
1/8 cup onion, diced
1/4 cup pumpkin seeds
Salt to taste
White pepper to taste
1 tablespoon butter
1 cup Mexican blend cheese, grated

Garnish:
Cayenne pepper

White Sauce
Melt the butter in a heavy saucepan. Stir in the flour and cook, stirring constantly until it makes a paste, but do not let it brown. Add the chicken broth, and continue to stir until the sauce thickens. Bring to a boil. Add salt, pepper and Serrano chili to taste. Lower heat and continue cooking for 2 to 3 minutes longer. Remove from heat, cover and set aside.

Personal
touches . . .

_____

_____

_____

_____

_____

_____

Enchiladas

Pour the corn oil in a frying pan and warm over medium heat. Fry the tortillas 1 at a time for 30 seconds on each side; do not allow tortillas to get crisp. Remove from oil and pat dry on a paper towel. Stack on a plate and set aside. In a separate bowl, combine eggs, squash, onion, pumpkin seeds, salt and pepper. Melt butter in a frying pan over medium heat. Pour egg mixture into pan and scramble, stirring mixture constantly. When eggs are ready, remove from burner and set aside. For each serving, place 1 tortilla on a serving plate. Spoon 1/4 of the eggs on each tortilla and sprinkle with cheese. Roll the tortilla up similar to a burrito. Ladle 1/4 of the white sauce over the top and sprinkle with more cheese. Garnish with cayenne pepper.

Servings: 4

Presented by: Hughes Hacienda Bed & Breakfast - Colorado Springs, Colorado

Personal touches . . .

Sausage Strata

1 pound Jimmy Dean® bulk sausage, hot
   (if using regular add 18 teaspoons dried pepper flakes)
6 extra large eggs
1 teaspoon prepared yellow mustard (not dry)
Salt to taste
Pepper to taste
3 cups milk
6 slices white bread (including crust)
2 cups sharp Cheddar cheese, grated
   (can substitute 1 cup sharp Cheddar cheese
   and 1 cup Monterey Jack cheese)

Garnish:
1 carrot, shredded
Fresh parsley sprigs

Use a Dutch oven or deep fry pan to brown sausage. While browning, use a wire whisk to smash any large clumps into tiny, even pieces. Drain sausage. In a large mixing bowl, beat eggs well; add mustard, salt and pepper, whisking until combined. Add milk, and mix well. Tear bread into small pieces and add to egg mixture; add cheese and drained sausage. Place ball of whisk, end down into the mixture, use an up-and-down motion until ingredients are well combined. When the bread is completely broken up, pour into an ungreased 9.5 x 13.5 (3-quart) glass baking dish. Cover and refrigerate overnight. The following morning, preheat oven to 350 degrees. Place pan on the center rack of oven and bake 30 to 35 minutes or until top and sides are slightly browned. Garnish with shredded carrot and a sprig of fresh parsley.

We served this to our very first guest 16 years ago. It's still a favorite and great for large groups. Doubles or triples easily.

Servings: 8

Presented by: The Breeden Inn Bed & Breakfast - Bennettsville, South Carolina

Personal touches . . .

Dutch Eggs

1/4 cup all-purpose flour
1 teaspoon baking powder
12 eggs
2 cups cottage cheese
4 tablespoons (1/2 stick) butter, melted
1 pound Monterey Jack cheese, grated

Preheat oven to 350 degrees and spray a 9 x 13 pan with non-stick cooking spray. In a large bowl, combine flour, baking powder and 2 eggs. Beat until mixture is thoroughly combined and smooth in texture. Add remaining 10 eggs, and beat until mixture is combined. Add cottage cheese, butter and Monterey Jack cheese, stirring until well combined. Pour mixture into pre-greased pan and bake for 50 minutes. The egg dish should be puffed and solid. Remove from oven and cool for 10 minutes. Cut into portions and serve.

To freeze: cool the dish completely and wrap in foil.
To reheat: thaw overnight in refrigerator, unwrap and microwave until hot.

Servings: 12

Presented by: Katherine's Bed & Breakfast -
Asheville, North Carolina

helpful hints . . .

In France, the term "oeufs en cocotte" is the basic method of baking eggs. Individual servings of baked eggs should be prepared in baking dishes (ramekins, custard cups, individual soufflé dishes or small oval bakers) that just fit the eggs plus the flavoring, food or liquid. If baking the eggs in other solid foods or in liquids, preheating the baking dishes before adding the eggs results in faster, more even cooking.

Personal touches . . .

omelettes

Did you know . . . asparagus is one of the lily family's cultivated forms. The optimum time of year for fresh asparagus is February through June, although hothouse asparagus is available year-round in some regions. Although best when cooked the same day it is purchased, it will keep three to four days if tightly wrapped in a plastic bag in the refrigerator. It can also be stored upright in a container with about an inch of water and covered with a plastic bag.

Personal touches . . .

Fresh Herb & Asparagus Baked Omelette

Top with Fresh Vegetable Salsa found on page 88

1 teaspoon butter/margarine to grease pie plate
5 to 6 stalks fresh asparagus, cut into 1-inch pieces
1 shallot, finely minced
1 teaspoon butter
8 eggs
1/2 cup milk
1 teaspoon fresh dill, finely chopped
2 tablespoons fresh parsley, finely chopped
1 tablespoon fresh chives, finely chopped
Salt to taste
Pepper to taste

Preheat oven to 350 degrees. Position rack in center of oven, and lightly grease 9-inch glass pie plate with butter or margarine. Steam asparagus for 2 to 3 minutes until tender and bright green in color. Spread in greased pie plate. Sauté shallot in butter until translucent. Sprinkle evenly over asparagus. In a medium bowl, mix eggs well with milk. Add herbs, salt and pepper. Pour over asparagus and shallots. Bake for 25 minutes or until set.

Servings: 6

Presented by: Forgett-Me-Nott Bed & Breakfast - Victoria, British Columbia

Leek, Herb and Ricotta Omelette

Did you know . . . you should always prepare several individual omelettes rather than one large omelette. You'll find each will be lighter, fluffier and easier to handle.

1 tablespoon butter
2 large eggs
Splash of half & half
Salt to taste
Pepper to taste
1 teaspoon thyme, chopped
2 to 3 tablespoons leeks, washed,
    sliced and sautéed in butter until soft
2 to 3 tablespoons ricotta cheese
Parmesan cheese, grated

Garnish:
Thyme or parsley

Heat a small omelette pan to medium heat and add butter. In a medium bowl, whisk together eggs, half & half, salt, pepper and thyme. When butter is foaming, add this mixture to pan. Stir eggs using a rubber spatula until they begin to set. Turn down the heat and cook slowly until lightly brown underneath. Sprinkle eggs with leeks, followed by the ricotta and Parmesan cheese. Place under broiler to set top and slightly melt ricotta. This should only take 1 to 2 minutes. Fold in thirds, place on plate and sprinkle with chopped thyme or parsley.

Servings: 1 per person

Presented by: Henry Whipple House Bed & Breakfast - Bristol, New Hampshire

Personal touches . . .

helpful hints . . .

The proper pan is very important for successful omelette making. If too large a pan is used, the high heat necessary cannot be maintained and cooking will be prolonged, resulting in a tough omelette. A 6- or 8-egg omelette can be prepared in an electric frying pan, as it provides an even source of heat.

Did you know . . . sherry is a fortified wine originally made in and around the town of Jerez in the Andalusia region of southern Spain. It is now also made in the United States and other parts of the world such as Australia and South Africa. It is most commonly used in cooking but can also be drunk. Dry sherries are usually drunk chilled, while sweet sherries are normally served at room temperature.

Personal touches . . .

_____

_____

_____

_____

_____

_____

Boursin and Tomato Omelette with Sherried Cream Mushrooms

6 tablespoons butter
8 ounces baby bella mushrooms
6 ounces medium dry sherry
1/3 cup heavy cream
8 eggs
1/2 cup milk
Cracked pepper blend to taste
2 roma tomatoes
4 ounces boursin cheese

Garnish:
Fresh chives

Sherried Cream Mushrooms
Melt 1 tablespoon butter, and coat bottom and sides of a 10-inch frying pan. Heat butter on medium and add mushrooms. Cook uncovered for 6 to 7 minutes until moisture from mushrooms coats bottom of pan. Add 2 tablespoons butter and increase heat, lightly stirring mushrooms frequently. Mushrooms should begin to brown on edges after an additional 2 to 3 minutes. When mushrooms have browned evenly, reduce heat to low and add 1 more tablespoon of butter; stir to coat all mushrooms. Allow pan to cool for 1 minute and return to burner. Add sherry and stir to coat all mushrooms. Pour heavy cream evenly over all mushrooms and stir to mix with sherry. Allow sherry/cream mixture to thicken slightly and remove from heat. Set aside until omelettes are ready.

Omelette
In a large mixing bowl, whisk eggs until foamy. Add milk and pepper, blend to taste. Continue to whisk until well blended. Melt 2 tablespoons of butter, and brush evenly on bottom and sides of 4 (8-inch) omelette pans. Place pans on burners set to medium. Distribute omelette mixture evenly among each pan. While omelettes set, slice tomatoes into thin rounds approximately 1/8-inch thick.

Remove boursin cheese from wrapper, and place on microwave-safe plate. Soften cheese slightly in microwave, approximately 15 seconds. When omelette mixture begins to bubble, use a spatula to pierce and lift cooked portions; allow loose mixture to flow into openings. Tilt pan to facilitate the flow of loose egg mixture. When egg mixture is set (but still moist), use a very thin long-blade spatula to separate omelette from pan edge. Move spatula fully under omelette, tilt pan so omelette slides onto spatula and quickly flip omelette over. Return pan to burner and turn off heat. Repeat for each omelette. Spread 1/4 of boursin cheese onto 1/2 of each omelette. Place 4 tomato slices on top of cheese. Fold empty side of omelette onto tomato/cheese mixture. Slide omelette onto serving plate and top with 1/4 of mushrooms. Use additional tomato slices and chives to garnish plate.

Servings: 4

Presented by: The Painted Lady Bed and Breakfast - Elmira, New York

Personal touches . . .

_____

_____

_____

_____

_____

_____

Did you know. . .
traditional omelettes
are savory but they
can also be made
sweet. Sweet
omelettes are filled
with custard, jelly or
fruit, sprinkled with
confectioners' sugar
or flamed with
assorted liqueurs
and liquors.

Baked Omelette

3 tablespoons butter
18 eggs
1 cup milk
1 cup sour cream
1 cup Cheddar cheese, shredded
1 teaspoon salt
Pepper to taste

Preheat oven to 350 degrees and melt butter in a 9 x 13 greased baking dish. Combine remaining ingredients in blender and mix well. Pour into hot baking dish. Bake for 30 minutes.

Meats and vegetables may be added if desired.

Servings: 10

Presented by: John F. Craig House - Cape May, New Jersey

Personal
touches . . .

_____

_____

_____

_____

_____

_____

quiche

Spinach Sausage Quiche

1/2 pound bulk sausage
1/4 cup green onion, chopped
1 clove garlic, minced
1 – 10 ounce package frozen chopped spinach,
    thawed and drained
1/2 cup herb stuffing mix
1 – 9-inch piecrust (unbaked)
1-1/2 cups Monterey Jack cheese, shredded
3 eggs, mixed
1-1/2 cups half & half
2 tablespoons Parmesan cheese
Paprika

Preheat oven to 375 degrees. Brown the sausage, onion
and garlic in a skillet and drain. Add the spinach and the
stuffing mix. Cover the bottom of pie shell with the
Monterey Jack cheese. Top with the sausage mixture. In
a separate bowl, combine the eggs and half & half. Pour
over sausage. Bake for 30 minutes. Sprinkle with
Parmesan cheese and paprika and bake for an additional
15 minutes, longer if necessary. Knife inserted should
come out clean. Let stand 10 minutes before serving.
Freezes and microwaves well for reheating.

Servings: 6

Presented by: 1831 Zachariah Eddy House Bed & Breakfast -
Middleboro, Massachusetts

Did you know . . .
to remove onion
or garlic odor from
your hands, place
your fingers on the
handle of a stainless
steel spoon and run
cold water over them.
The smell will
immediately
disappear.

Personal
touches . . .

_____
_____
_____
_____
_____
_____
_____

Hacienda Quiche

1 – 9-inch piecrust (Pillsbury®), unbaked
2 tablespoons butter
2 cups fresh mushrooms, chopped
1 teaspoon garlic, crushed
6 eggs
1 cup heavy whipping cream
1 tablespoon Worcestershire sauce
1 tablespoon sugar
1/2 teaspoon salt
1/8 teaspoon freshly ground pepper
1/2 teaspoon onion salt
2 cups Swiss cheese, grated
1 bunch fresh spinach, chopped,
   or one (10-ounce) package frozen chopped spinach,
   thawed and squeezed dry

Preheat oven to 350 degrees. Prepare piecrust according to instructions on the package. In a skillet, melt the butter and sauté the mushrooms over medium heat until soft. Add the garlic and continue to sauté briefly, do not burn; set aside.

Personal touches . . .

_____

_____

_____

_____

_____

_____

_____

Store mushrooms in the refrigerator in an open paper bag or basket. Air circulation is important to maintain dryness. Because excess moisture will cause them to spoil faster, do not clean the mushrooms until you're ready to use them.

In a large mixing bowl, combine eggs, cream, Worcestershire sauce, sugar, salt, pepper and onion salt. Whip mixture with a whisk until smooth, and then mix in cheese. Layer the bottom of the piecrust with the mushrooms and spinach; pour egg mixture over the top. Bake for 40 minutes or until knife inserted comes out clean. Remove from oven and let stand 10 minutes before serving.

Servings: 6 to 8

Presented by: Hughes Hacienda Bed & Breakfast - Colorado Springs, Colorado

Did you know . . .
quiche originated in
northeastern France
in the region of
Alsace-Lorraine.
Ingredients consist of
a pastry shell filled
with a savory custard
made of eggs, cream,
seasonings and
various other
ingredients. Not only
a breakfast dish,
quiche can be served
as a lunch or dinner
entrée, a first course
or hors d'oeuvres.

Personal
touches . . .

_____

_____

_____

_____

_____

_____

_____

Crustless Three-Cheese Quiche

6 large eggs
4 large egg yolks
1 cup half & half
1 cup heavy whipping cream
1/2 teaspoon Mrs. Dash®, Riley's® or similar seasoning
1 cup sharp Cheddar cheese, shredded
2/3 cup Monterey Jack cheese, grated
1/3 cup Swiss cheese, grated
2 teaspoons fresh parsley, chopped

Preheat oven to 350 degrees. Spray bottom of 10-inch quiche dish with non-stick spray. In medium mixing bowl, combine eggs and yolks, half & half, heavy cream and seasoning. Whisk to combine. Reserve a couple of pinches of Cheddar cheese and add remaining cheeses to the liquid mixture; blend with whisk. Pour mixture into the sprayed quiche dish. Sprinkle reserved Cheddar and parsley on top. Bake for 40 to 50 minutes or until knife inserted in the center comes out clean.

Servings: 6 to 7

Presented by: Reagan's Queen Anne Bed and Breakfast - Hannibal, Missouri

Personal touches . . .

_____

_____

_____

_____

_____

_____

_____

helpful hints . . .

Parsley is usually sold in bunches and should be chosen for its bright green leaves that show no sign of wilting. To store fresh parsley, wash and shake off excess moisture. Then wrap the bunch in paper towels and place in a plastic bag. Fresh parsley can be refrigerated for up to a week.

Arrington's Inn Traveler® is a quarterly publication dedicated to the sophisticated bed & breakfast and country inn traveler. It is fast becoming the premier bed & breakfast and country inn publication of its kind. Each issue showcases 20 properties throughout the United States and Canada, delving into the history of the establishment, the amenities offered, room descriptions and the elaborate meals offered by each property. In addition to the detailed bed & breakfast and country inn features, area attractions for each establishment are highlighted to assist you in planning your next trip.

Other useful information such as products, travel advice from various experts and signature recipes are offered with each issue. If you are a seasoned, sophisticated inngoer or planning your first B&B experience, let *Arrington's Inn Traveler®* be your passport to luxury.

YES! Send me Arrington's Inn Traveler®!

☐   1 year (4 issues) only $10.00   ☐   2 years (8 issues) only $15.00

Texas Residents 1 year - $10.83, 2 years - $16.24
Canadian Residents 1 year - $15.00, 2 years - $20.00

Name _

Address _ _ _ _ _ _ _ _ _ _ _ _ _ _ _ _ _ _ _ Apt. _ _ _ _ _ _ _ _ _ _ _ _

City _ State _ _ _ _ _ _ Zip _ _ _ _

E-mail _

Payment Enclosed ☐   Bill Me Later ☐

Remit to:
Arrington Publishing, 214 W. Texas, Suite 400, Midland, Texas 79701

Breads

pancakes

David's International Pancakes

Buttermilk pancake mix
1 very ripe banana, South American recommended
1/3 cup fresh California walnuts, chopped
1 teaspoon Mexican vanilla

Using any buttermilk pancake mix, prepare as directed for serving 4 people. Add 1 large banana to the batter. The trick here is to purchase the overripe bananas from your local produce stand; store in freezer. On the morning that you wish to serve, remove bananas from freezer, microwave for about 30 seconds or until thawed. Cut the end off, and squeeze out the meat with the juices into the batter. Add walnuts and vanilla. Blend well and let stand for 30 minutes to set the flavors. Cook the pancakes on a preheated griddle and serve with Canadian maple syrup, crisp bacon and fruit juice.

Servings: 4

Presented by: A Rover's Rest Bed and Breakfast -
Blind Bay, British Columbia

Personal
touches . . .

Baked Apple Pancakes

Pancakes:
1/2 cup milk
1/2 cup all-purpose flour
1/2 teaspoon baking soda
3 eggs
1 teaspoon sugar
Dash of salt

Apples:
3 tablespoons butter
1/4 cup sugar
4 Granny Smith apples, peeled, cored and sliced
1/3 cup dried cranberries
1/3 cup walnuts, chopped
Sprinkle of cinnamon sugar
Dab of butter
Canned whip cream

Garnish:
Fresh mint sprigs
Cinnamon sticks

Preheat oven to 400 degrees and spray an 8-inch cake pan with non-stick cooking spray. In a small bowl, mix all of the pancake ingredients together until smooth; set aside. Melt butter in a large skillet over medium high heat. Mix in sugar, apples, dried cranberries and walnuts. Sauté apple mixture for about 5 minutes until soft but not mushy. Place 1/2 of apple mixture in bottom of cake pan. Pour pancake batter over apples. Bake 10 minutes. Remove from oven, sprinkle with cinnamon sugar and top with a dab of butter. Return to oven and bake for an additional 15 minutes. To serve, place pancakes on individual serving plates while hot. Spoon remaining apples over each serving. Top with dollops of whip cream. Garnish with a fresh mint sprig and cinnamon stick.

Personal touches . . .

_____

_____

_____

_____

_____

_____

This dish can be baked and served in several ways. The whole recipe in a 9-inch layer cake pan can be served whole or in half as a breakfast entrée for one or two people. It can also be cut in 6 wedges as individual servings or baked in 4 to 6 individual custard dishes.

Servings: 2 to 6

Presented by: 1831 Zachariah Eddy House Bed & Breakfast - Middleboro, Massachusetts

helpful hints . . .

Apples that are great for eating fresh are not necessarily ideal for cooking. The heat from cooking breaks down their texture. They become less flavorful as well as mushy and soggy in texture. The list below includes the best uses for the most widely available types of apples.

Baking and Pies:
> Braeburn
> Rome Beauty
> York Imperial

Fresh Treats and Salads:
> Cortland
> Empire
> Gala
> McIntosh
> Newtown Pippin
> Northern Spy
> Red Delicious
> Stayman

All-Purpose:
> Crispin
> Criterion
> Fuji
> Golden Delicious
> Granny Smith
> Jonagold
> Jonathan
> Winesap

Personal touches . . .

From the words of Shakespeare . . .
"Of a certain knight, that swore by his honor they were good pancakes, and wore by his honor the mustard was naught. Now I'll stand to it, the pancakes were naught, and the mustard was good, and yet was not the knight forsworn." As You Like It (1.02 64-67)

Personal touches . . .

_____

_____

_____

_____

_____

_____

Cottage Cheese Pancakes with Fruit Sauce

These are great because they are simple, take very little time to make, can be prepared well ahead of time, will last for days and, most of all, they are delicious!

Fruit Sauce:
2-1/2 cups apple juice
3/4 cup sugar
2 tablespoons corn starch
1 bag frozen fruit of your choice

Pancakes:
2 cups low-fat cottage cheese
2 large eggs
1/4 cup sugar
1 tablespoon lemon juice
Pinch salt
1 cup flour
3 tablespoons butter, melted
3 tablespoons oil
Dab of sour cream

Fruit Sauce
Heat 2 cups of apple juice and sugar in a saucepan, stirring until sugar dissolves (reserve 1/2 cup of apple juice to add in next step). Dissolve cornstarch in reserved juice and then add to the apple/sugar mixture. Keep on heat and stir constantly until thickened. Take off heat and add frozen fruit, stirring until fruit has softened. Sauce can be served immediately, or it can be chilled and served later, either warm or cold depending upon its use.

Pancakes

Whip cottage cheese until creamy (food processor works best for removing all lumps). Add eggs, sugar, lemon juice and salt. Mix well and add flour until batter thickens. Refrigerate until ready to cook. Batter may be prepared 1 or 2 days in advance. When ready to cook, brush hot griddle or non-stick skillet with butter and/or oil. Drop batter by tablespoons to make pancakes about 3 inches in diameter. When bottom is lightly browned and bubbles have formed on surface, turn over and brown other side. Serve 2 cakes with Fruit Sauce and a dab of sour cream.

Servings: 4 to 6

Presented by: Morning Glory Inn - Slatyfork, West Virginia

From the words of Shakespeare . . .
"As fit as ten groats for the hand of an attorney, as your French crown for you taffeta punk, as Tib's rush for Tom's forefinger, as a pancake for Shrove Tuesday, a morris for May-day, as the nail to his hole, the cockold to his horn, as a scolding quean to a wrangling knave, as the nun's lip to the friar's mouth, nay, as the pudding to his skin."
All's Well that Ends Well (2.02 23)

Personal touches . . .

_____

_____

_____

_____

_____

_____

_____

*Did you know . . .
in Sweden, a typical
Thursday supper
includes pea soup,
broiled pork and a
dessert of pancakes.
The pancakes, also
known as "plattar,"
are usually served
with jam or
lingonberries. This
meal combination has
been a tradition for
Swedish families
since the Middle
Ages.*

Denison House Pancakes

Edward Denison built our home in 1710, and these pancakes were named for him.

2 cups flour
2 teaspoons baking powder
1/2 teaspoon salt
1 tablespoon powdered sugar
2 eggs, well beaten
1-3/4 cups milk (about)
1 teaspoon vanilla

In a bowl, combine dry ingredients. In a separate bowl, combine eggs, milk and vanilla, and beat with a hand whisk until color is uniform. Add flour mixture and whisk until smooth. More milk may be necessary to thin the batter, especially if it sits for more than a few minutes.

Heat a nonstick fry pan or griddle over medium heat and drop 1/4 cup of batter onto pan. Turn when bubbles cover the surface and bottom is golden brown. Remove from pan when golden brown on both sides and repeat procedure. Serve with butter or your favorite syrup, preferably heated for the best flavor!

Servings: 6 (2 pancakes per person)

Presented by: Another Second Penny Inn - Stonington, Connecticut

*Personal
touches . . .*

_____

_____

_____

_____

_____

_____

_____

Cocoa Pancakes with Caramel Banana Sauce

Caramel Banana Sauce:
3/4 cup packed brown sugar
1/2 cup milk
2 tablespoons butter or margarine
2 teaspoons vanilla extract
4 to 5 medium bananas, sliced diagonally

Pancakes:
2 eggs
1-1/2 cups milk
2 tablespoons canola oil
2 cups flour
1/4 cup sugar
4 tablespoons cocoa
2 teaspoons baking powder

Caramel Banana Sauce
Combine all of sauce ingredients except for bananas in saucepan. Heat to boiling over medium heat, stirring occasionally. Remove from heat and stir in banana slices gently until coated.

Pancakes
Preheat griddle to 350 degrees. In a mixing bowl, beat eggs until foamy, beat in milk and oil. Add remaining ingredients, stirring until batter is smooth. Spoon batter onto hot griddle. Cook both sides until golden brown. Serve with warm Caramel Banana Sauce.

Servings: 4 to 6

Presented by: Millcreek Homestead Bed & Breakfast - Bird-in-Hand, Pennsylvania

Did you know . . . an average banana packs a healthy punch with about 602 mg of potassium, only 140 calories, 2 grams of protein, 4 grams of fiber, 2 mg sodium, 36 grams of carbohydrates and an abundance of vitamins and minerals. They are high in iron and recommended by doctors for those with anemia. Bananas also contain tryptophan, a type of protein that is converted by the body into serotonin, which is known to generally improve moods and happiness.

Personal touches . . .

french toast

Did you know . . .
canned peaches are
either peeled, yellow
clingstone or
freestone varieties.
They are available as
halves, quarters,
slices or diced. They
are packed in
unsweetened fruit
juice, light syrup,
lightly sweetened
fruit juice and water.

Personal
touches . . .

_____

_____

_____

_____

_____

_____

_____

Peach Melba French Toast

1 cup brown sugar
1 stick butter
2 tablespoons maple syrup
1 (29-ounce) can sliced peaches, drained
5 eggs
1-1/2 cups half & half
1 tablespoon vanilla
1 loaf challah or Portuguese sweet bread,
　 sliced 1 inch thick
Cinnamon
Sugar

Pre-grease a 13 x 9 baking pan or dish. In a small saucepan, combine brown sugar, butter and maple syrup and heat on medium until mixture becomes thick and foamy. Pour mixture into baking pan or dish. Place peaches along the bottom of the pan evenly. Lay bread slices closely together over peaches. In a small mixing bowl, beat eggs, half & half and vanilla. Pour mixture over bread, making sure each slice is thoroughly saturated with liquid. Cover and refrigerate overnight. The next morning, preheat oven to 450 degrees. Uncover dish and place in oven. Bake 40 minutes. Remove from oven. Place large platter on a flat surface and securely flip baking dish over onto platter. This is similar to how you make Pineapple Upside Down Cake. The peaches and caramel should be on top.

Servings: 6

Presented by: Wander Inn - Newport, Rhode Island

Decadent Southern Stuffed French Toast

6 ounces ricotta cheese
6 ounces cream cheese
1/4 cup pecans, chopped
1/3 cup sugar
1 teaspoon vanilla extract
1/2 teaspoon lemon zest
2 loaves French bread
6 eggs
1-3/4 cups half & half
1-1/4 cups orange juice, reduced
1 teaspoon orange extract
1/3 cup sugar
1/2 cup blueberries
Cornstarch to thicken

Garnish:
Blueberries, pecans, whipped cream

In a medium mixing bowl, whip ricotta and cream cheese, pecans, sugar, vanilla extract and lemon zest. Fold mixture into pastry bag and set aside. Slice French bread 1-1/2 inches thick and at an angle. Cut pockets in each slice to hold filling. Squeeze enough filling mixture to fill each pocket. In a separate bowl, combine eggs and half & half. Soak each slice in egg mixture. Preheat a griddle to medium high. When griddle is heated, spray with cooking oil and then place bread slices on heated surface to fry. Fry both sides until golden brown, 2 to 3 minutes on each side. Place bread slices on a platter and cover with foil. Set in oven to maintain warmth. In a small saucepan, combine orange juice, orange extract, sugar, blueberries and cornstarch. Warm ingredients over medium heat and stir until sauce begins to thicken. Remove sauce from heat. Serve 2 to 3 slices of bread garnished with blueberries, pecans and a dollop of whipped cream. Serve sauce on the side for dipping or pouring over individual plates.

Servings: 6

Presented by: Inn at the Bay Bed & Breakfast - St. Petersburg, Florida

helpful hints . . .

when choosing fresh oranges, look for fruit that is firm and heavy for its size. The fruit should not have any mold or spongy spots. Oranges should only be kept at room temperature for a day or two and then stored in the refrigerator to maintain freshness. Oranges will stay good in the refrigerator for up to two weeks.

Personal touches . . .

Did you know . . . French toast is a common breakfast dish prepared by dipping bread into an egg and milk combination, then frying it until golden brown on both sides. Traditional serving varieties include syrup, jam or powdered sugar. The French term for French toast is "pain perdu" (lost bread). This term is used because the process of cooking French toast is a way of reviving French bread, which becomes dry after only a day or two.

Personal touches . . .

_____

_____

_____

_____

_____

_____

_____

Baked Coconut Cinnamon French Toast

1/2 stick butter, softened
8 ounces cream cheese, softened
1/2 cup maple syrup, divided in half
1 large loaf cinnamon raisin bread,
   sliced into fingerlike pieces
8 large eggs
2-1/2 cups milk
1/2 teaspoon vanilla extract
1/4 cup coconut
Walnuts (optional)
4 to 5 tablespoons brown sugar
Cinnamon
Powdered sugar

Mix butter, cream cheese and half of the maple syrup. Heat in microwave until softened to a creamy texture, making sure to eliminate all lumps by mixing well with a whisk.

Place sliced raisin bread evenly in a well-buttered 13 x 9 glass baking dish. Spread some cream cheese mixture on top of the bread slices, leaving room for the egg mixture to be absorbed through the cream cheese mixture. Beat the eggs, milk, remaining maple syrup and vanilla. Pour over the bread, and sprinkle with the coconut and walnuts. Sprinkle brown sugar and cinnamon on top of the bread dish. Cover with aluminum foil and refrigerate overnight. Uncover and bake for 40 to 50 minutes at 350 degrees. Cut into rectangles and serve on plates drizzled with maple syrup and sprinkled with powdered sugar. Serve hot.

Servings: 10

Presented by: The Dutch Iris Inn Bed & Breakfast - Granby, Connecticut

Stuffed French Toast a l'orange

1 cup cream cheese, softened
2 to 3 tablespoons orange juice
16 slices French Bread, 1 inch in thickness
4 eggs
3/4 cup milk
1/8 teaspoon vanilla
3/4 teaspoon orange zest
Nutmeg
1 tablespoon cooking oil
16 mandarin orange segments
Powdered sugar

Blend cream cheese with orange juice. Spread mixture on 8 slices of bread. Top with remaining 8 slices of bread. Mix egg, milk, vanilla and orange zest. Dip "sandwiches" in egg mixture. Place on platter and lightly sprinkle with nutmeg. Heat oil in skillet or griddle. Cook "sandwiches" until golden brown on both sides. Place 2 orange segments on each "sandwich," sprinkle with powdered sugar and serve.

Servings: 4

Presented by: Pikes Peak Paradise Bed and Breakfast - Woodland Park, Colorado

Did you know . . . spices such as nutmeg, and herbs such as parsley, played a dramatic role in the development and advancement of Western civilization. During ancient and medieval times, spices were rare and precious commodities used for flavorings, incense, perfumes and medicines. The Queen of Sheba used spices, precious stones and gold to make a tribute to King Solomon. The first Olympians in Greece celebrated their victory by wearing wreaths of parsley and bay.

Personal touches . . .

_____
_____
_____
_____
_____
_____
_____

helpful hints . . .

"Icing sugar" is the British term for confectioners' sugar. If you discover you are without confectioners' sugar while baking, use 1/2 cup and 1 tablespoon of granulated sugar for every 1 cup of confectioners' sugar as a substitution.

Stuffed French Toasted Croissants

1/2 cup cream cheese, softened
1/2 cup bananas, finely diced
1/2 cup fresh strawberries, finely diced
1/4 cup fresh pineapple, finely diced
4 large croissants, sliced in half horizontally,
    leaving two inches of the outside curve
    of croissant intact
3 large eggs
2 tablespoons cream
2 to 3 tablespoons butter for frying
Icing sugar (confectioners' sugar)
Toasted sliced almonds

Blend softened cream cheese gently with bananas, strawberries and pineapple until well mixed. Spread 1/4 cream cheese filling inside each croissant. Beat eggs lightly, add cream and mix well. Dip stuffed croissants into egg mixture and fry in butter on medium high heat until golden brown, 2 to 3 minutes on each side. Slice in half vertically, dust with icing sugar and sprinkle with toasted sliced almonds. Serve with your favorite syrup, fruit purée or sauce.

Servings: 4

Presented by: Forgett-Me-Nott Bed & Breakfast - Victoria, British Columbia

Personal touches . . .

"I Couldn't Eat Another Bite" Stuffed French Toast

6 to 7 large eggs
1 cup French vanilla coffee creamer
1/2 teaspoon nutmeg
3 cups cornflake cereal, crushed to 1 cup
1/2 cup unsweetened coconut, shredded
8 ounces Tofutti® imitation cream cheese
2 teaspoons vanilla
2 tablespoons Splenda® or fructose
8 tablespoons hazelnuts, coarsely chopped
1 large loaf French bread

Preheat griddle to 325 degrees. Combine and blend eggs, French vanilla coffee creamer and nutmeg in a bowl; set aside. In a flat pan with sides, combine cornflakes and coconut; set aside. Combine cream cheese, vanilla, Splenda® and hazelnuts; set aside. Create pockets in the French bread by cutting through the top and along one side of each bread slice. Each portion should be about 1 inch thick. Spread a rounded tablespoon (1 to 2 spoonfuls, depending on the size of the bread loaf) of the cream cheese filling inside each pocket. Dip each bread portion into egg/creamer mixture, then press into corn flake/coconut mixture. Lightly coat both sides. Cook on lightly greased griddle until golden on each side. If bread portion seems too soft, stand pieces on edge and cook edges as well as the sides. Extra cream cheese mixture may be used as a toast spread.

Servings: 8

Presented by: A Creekside Garden Inn - Salem, Oregon

Did you know . . . Tofutti® is a brand of soy-based dairy free products that provide a tasty healthful alternative to dairy products such as ice cream, sour cream and cream cheese. Tofutti® products are available at many major supermarkets and health food stores. Check their Web site www.tofutti.com for product availability in your area.

Personal touches . . .

_____

_____

_____

_____

_____

_____

_____

*Did you know . . .
one of the earliest
recorded recipes for a
dish similar to
French toast was by
Bartolomeo de Sacchi
di Piadena. Piadena,
also known as
"Platina," during the
15th century wrote
"De Honesta
Voluptate", which
included his opinions
and views concerning
food, spices and
various other
culinary elements.
He discussed both
their culinary and
medicinal uses. The
recipe describes a
dish of bread soaked
in an egg batter and
then fried.*

*Personal
touches . . .*

_____

_____

_____

_____

_____

_____

_____

Apple Cinnamon Baked French Toast

1 large loaf French bread
8 extra large eggs
1 cup sugar
3-1/2 cups milk
1 tablespoon vanilla
6 to 8 cooking apples such as Macintosh or Cortland,
    peeled, cored and sliced
3 teaspoons cinnamon
1 teaspoon nutmeg
1 stick butter

Slice bread into 1-1/2-inch thick slices. Spray a 9 x 13 glass pan with non-stick spray. Place bread tightly in dish. In a separate bowl, beat together eggs, 1/2 cup sugar, milk and vanilla with whisk. Pour half of mixture over bread. Place apples on top of bread to cover. Pour remaining milk mixture over bread. Mix remaining 1/2 cup sugar with cinnamon and nutmeg and sprinkle over the top of apples. Dot with butter, cover and refrigerate overnight. In the morning, preheat oven to 350 degrees. Uncover dish and bake in oven for 1 hour. It will rise high and brown nicely. Remove from oven and allow to rest for 5 to 10 minutes before serving. Cut into squares and serve with heated syrup and your favorite meat entrée.

Servings: 10 to 12

Presented by: The Homeridge Bed and Breakfast - Jerseyville, Illinois

Baked Caramel French Toast

Topping:
1 cup brown sugar, packed
1/3 cup heavy cream
6 tablespoons butter
1 tablespoon light corn syrup
1/2 cup pecans (optional)

French Toast:
4 large eggs
1 teaspoon vanilla extract
1/2 cup milk
1/4 teaspoon salt
1/4 teaspoon nutmeg
8 – 3/4-inch thick slices of French bread

Spray a 9 x 13 baking dish with non-stick cooking spray. In a medium saucepan, combine topping ingredients, mix well. Cook over low-medium heat until bubbly, stirring constantly. Remove from heat immediately and pour into sprayed baking dish. Set aside. You may add an optional 1/2 cup of pecans to caramel at this point. In a shallow mixing bowl, beat eggs, vanilla, milk, salt and nutmeg. Dip each bread slice in mixture, making sure that all of the liquid is used by all 8 pieces. Place dipped bread over caramel mixture in dish. Cover tightly and refrigerate for 8 hours or overnight. When ready to bake, allow to sit for 20 to 30 minutes to warm to room temperature. Uncover and bake in 375-degree oven, on middle rack for 30 to 40 minutes until bubbly and golden brown. Make sure to watch carefully so that caramel does not burn. Cool for 5 minutes, then with large spatula keeping caramel in place, invert 2 pieces (each) onto serving plates. Spoon extra caramel from baking dish over toast and onto the plate. Serve immediately.

Servings: 4

Presented by: Reagan's Queen Anne Bed and Breakfast - Hannibal, Missouri

Did you know . . . aged bread is actually better for preparing French toast than fresh bread. It will absorb the egg/milk mixture better without crumbling or falling apart.

Personal touches . . .

———————————
———————————
———————————
———————————
———————————
———————————

*Did you know . . .
in England, French
toast is referred to as
"poor knights in
Windsor" or "poor
knights pudding"
and used as a means
to make use of crusts
and stale, aged bread.*

Chambord French Toast

10 croissants
2/3 cup raspberry preserves
1/3 cup orange juice
3 tablespoons Chambord
12 eggs
1 cup whole milk
3/4 cup heavy cream
1 pint fresh raspberries
Confectioners' sugar

Preheat oven to 350 degrees and spray pan or baking dish with non-stick cooking spray. Cut croissants into cubes, and arrange half of the cubes on the bottom of pan or baking dish. Mix together preserves, juice and Chambord. Pour on top of the croissant cubes. Put the other half of the croissant cubes on top. Combine eggs, milk and cream. Pour over croissant cubes. Scatter fresh raspberries on top. Bake 45 minutes. Sprinkle with confectioners' sugar before serving.

"This is pretty sweet, so I normally serve the maple syrup on the side. I also team it with more savory than sweet baked goods so as not to induce sugar comas in my guests. Crisp bacon, eggs, fresh fruit, homemade wheat bread and nutmeg muffins are perfect accompaniments." – Innkeeper Laurie Steets

Servings: 4 to 6

Presented by: The Evergreen Inn Bed & Breakfast - Spring Lake, New Jersey

*Personal
touches . . .*

morning breads

Camilla's Allison House Inn Banana Bread

1/2 cup shortening
1 cup sugar
2 eggs
2 cups flour
1 teaspoon baking soda
1/3 cup milk
1 teaspoon lemon juice
1 cup mashed bananas
1/2 cup walnuts, coarsely chopped (optional)

Preheat oven to 325 degrees, and grease and flour 2 small loaf pans. In a separate bowl, beat shortening, sugar and eggs. Combine flour and baking soda in an additional bowl and set aside. In a third bowl, combine milk, lemon juice, bananas and walnuts. Alternately add flour mixture and banana mixture to egg mixture until thoroughly combined. Fill loaf pans half full of batter and bake approximately 1 hour or until toothpick inserted comes out dry. The bread will be golden brown in color.

Servings: 2 loaves

Presented by: The Allison House Inn - Quincy, Florida

Did you know . . . February 23 is officially recognized as National Banana Bread Day. So celebrate!

Personal touches . . .

_____
_____
_____
_____
_____
_____
_____

Did you know . . . when making quick breads it is extremely important to measure each ingredient accurately. If you add too much liquid, the bread may sink, and if you add too much fat, the bread will be very course in texture. Dry measuring cups should be used for all dry ingredients such as flour or sugar. Liquid measuring cups should be used for all liquid ingredients. Measuring spoons are appropriate for use with small amounts of both dry and wet ingredients.

Judy's Apple Bread

1-1/2 cups canola oil
2 cups sugar
4 eggs
3 cups White Lily® plain flour
1 teaspoon baking soda
1 teaspoon cinnamon
1/2 teaspoon salt
1 teaspoon vanilla
2 cups Red Delicious apple (with peel), chopped
1 cup toasted pecans, chopped

Preheat oven to 325 degrees; butter and flour a 9 x 5 loaf pan. Mix all ingredients until just combined. Pour into loaf pan and bake for approximately 1-1/2 hours. Rotate pan halfway through baking time to ensure even baking. Cool completely in pan. Freezes very well and will stay moist for several days at room temperature.

Servings: 1 loaf

Presented by: Blair-Moore House Bed & Breakfast - Jonesborough, Tennessee

Personal touches . . .

_____

_____

_____

_____

_____

_____

Cinnamon Ring

Bread:
1 tablespoon yeast (1 packet)
1 teaspoon salt
1/4 cup shortening
1/3 cup powdered milk
1 egg
3 tablespoons sugar
3-1/2 to 4 cups flour
1-1/4 cups warm water

Filling:
3 tablespoons margarine
3 tablespoons brown sugar
3 tablespoons granulated sugar
1 teaspoon cinnamon
1/4 cup chopped pecans
Candied fruit (optional)

Combine all bread ingredients and put into bread machine. Press dough button (1 hour and 30 minutes). Divide into 2 parts. Roll out and spread with softened margarine. Layer brown sugar, granulated sugar, cinnamon, pecans and optional candied fruit on top of margarine. Roll into tube shape. Make a circle and join ends together. Place on a cookie sheet, and let rise 30 minutes. Bake at 350 degrees for 20 to 25 minutes. Cool and ice with your favorite icing.

Servings: 1 ring

Presented by: Lococo House II Bed & Breakfast -
St. Charles, Missouri

Did you know . . . brown sugar is the combination of white sugar and molasses. The most common varieties are light and dark. Usually, the lighter the brown sugar, the more subtle the molasses flavor. The darker variety, also known as "old-fashioned," tends to have a more concentrated molasses flavor. There are granulated and liquid brown sugars available, yet neither should be used as substitutions for standard brown sugar in recipes.

Personal touches . . .

_____

_____

_____

_____

_____

_____

_____

*Did you know . . .
recent medical
studies have revealed
that although small
in size, blueberries
have powerful
potential health
benefits that include
anti-aging effects,
anti-cancer activity,
aid in the prevention
of urinary tract
infections, reduction
of eyestrain and
improvement of
night vision.*

*Personal
touches . . .*

_____

_____

_____

_____

_____

_____

_____

Roaring Lion Wild Blueberry Muffins

1/2 cup butter or margarine
1 cup plus 1 teaspoon sugar (for sprinkling on top)
2 eggs
1 teaspoon vanilla
2 cups flour
2 teaspoons baking powder
1/2 teaspoon salt
1/2 cup milk
2 cups frozen blueberries

Cream the butter or margarine with sugar. Add eggs and vanilla and beat well. (From the innkeeper: I do all my mixing by hand, using a pastry cutter to cream the butter and sugar and for mixing in the eggs and vanilla. Then finish the mixing in of the dry ingredients with a rubber spatula.) Add the well mixed dry ingredients and milk and mix well. Get the blueberries from the freezer and mix them into the batter. Turn into lined cupcake tins. Sprinkle sugar over the top of each muffin. Bake for 25 to 30 minutes at 375 degrees.

Frozen cranberries can be used as a substitute for blueberries. Have the batter ready, take the cranberries from the freezer and roughly chop in food processor, and stir into batter.

Servings: 12

Presented by: The Roaring Lion Bed & Breakfast - Waldoboro, Maine

Nana's Banana Bread

2 eggs
1 cup sugar
1/2 cup butter
1 teaspoon vanilla
2 cups all-purpose flour
2 teaspoons baking powder
1 teaspoon baking soda
1/2 teaspoon cinnamon
4 tablespoons sour milk
2 ripe bananas
1 cup semi-sweet chocolate chips
1/2 cup coconut, shredded
1 cup walnuts, chopped
Cinnamon sugar for sprinkling
   (1/4 cup sugar combined with 1 teaspoon cinnamon)
Butter or softened cream cheese

Preheat oven to 350 degrees and spray a loaf pan with non-stick cooking spray. Cream eggs and sugar. Melt butter and slowly add to cream mixture. Add vanilla to cream mixture. Add flour and baking soda and powder to mixture. Alternately add sour milk and mashed bananas. Add chocolate chips, coconut and nuts. Make sure it is blended well. Pour into prepared pan. Sprinkle liberally with cinnamon sugar. Bake for 50 to 60 minutes. Test after 50 minutes with cake tester. Do not over bake. Let sit at least 20 minutes. Slice, and serve warm with butter or softened cream cheese.

Servings: 1 loaf (6 to 8 slices)

Presented by: Blair Manor - Stowe, Vermont

Personal touches . . .

_____

_____

_____

_____

_____

_____

helpful hints . . .

To make sour milk or a substitution for buttermilk, combine 4 teaspoons white vinegar or lemon juice to 1 cup of milk. Allow mixture to sit for at least 5 minutes before using.

*Did you know . . .
sweet monkey bread
can be made with
sugar, nuts,
cinnamon and/or
raisins and savory
monkey bread can be
made with cheese
and various herbs.
Monkey bread has a
unique loaf texture
created by arranging
small clumps of
dough, usually
dipped in butter, and
layered in a round,
oblong or tube-
shaped pan.*

Monkey Bread

2 cups pecans, chopped
1/2 cup butter
1 cup brown sugar
2 tablespoons water
2 cans flaky biscuits

Grease a tube or bundt pan. Sprinkle bottom of pan with 1-1/2 cups pecans. In a small saucepan, melt butter and add sugar, water and pecans. Set aside. Cut each biscuit into halves and form each half into a ball. You should have 40 balls. Place 20 balls in the bottom of the pan. Drizzle balls with half of the melted mixture. Place the remaining 20 balls in the pan and top with remaining mixture. Bake at 350 degrees for 20 to 25 minutes.

Servings: 10 to 12

Presented by: John F. Craig House - Cape May, New Jersey

*Personal
touches . . .*

Alaskan Rhubarb Coffeecake

Coffeecake:
1/2 cup butter
1-1/2 cups brown sugar
2 eggs
2 cups flour
1/2 teaspoon salt
1 teaspoon baking soda
1 cup buttermilk
1-1/2 cups chopped rhubarb, fresh or frozen

Topping:
1/2 cup sugar
1/2 cup nuts
1 teaspoon cinnamon

Cream butter and brown sugar. Add eggs and dry ingredients alternating with buttermilk. Fold rhubarb into batter; pour into 9 x 13 greased pan. Combine sugar, nuts and cinnamon, sprinkle over top. Bake at 350 degrees for 45 minutes.

Presented by: Alaska Gold Rush Bed & Breakfast - Palmer, Alaska

Personal touches . . .

helpful hints . . .

When baking coffeecakes, use a shiny metal pan for best results. It will reflect the heat better and produce a golden, tender crust. Coffeecakes are best when served warm. Allow coffeecake to cool for at least 20 to 30 minutes before serving.

crescents, crêpes & scones

Breeden Inn Cinnamon Crescents

1 can (8 ounces) Pillsbury® crescent rolls
4 tablespoons butter or margarine
1/2 cup pecans, walnuts or almonds, crushed
2 tablespoons cinnamon sugar
  (1/4 cup sugar combined with 1 teaspoon cinnamon)
1/2 teaspoon cinnamon
1 cup powdered sugar
Water or milk, just enough to thin icing

Preheat oven to 375 degrees. Unroll dough and separate into 8 individual sections on a cookie sheet. Melt butter or margarine. Add nuts and 1 tablespoon cinnamon sugar, reserving 1 tablespoon for final brushing. Heat through but do not boil or overcook. Sprinkle 1/2 tablespoon of cinnamon sugar over triangles. Place a tablespoon of the butter/nut mixture in the center of each triangle. Roll triangle from the shortest to the widest end. Place point side down, and fold sides under on an ungreased cookie sheet. Brush with remaining melted butter or margarine from saucepan. Sprinkle with cinnamon sugar. Bake for 8 to 10 minutes. Mix powdered sugar, 1/2 teaspoon of cinnamon with just enough water or milk to thin. Drizzle over each crescent. Sprinkle with remaining or additional cinnamon sugar.

Servings: 8

Presented by: The Breeden Inn Bed & Breakfast - Bennettsville, South Carolina

Personal touches . . .

_____

_____

_____

_____

_____

_____

Bass & Baskets Stuffed Crescents

8 ounces cream cheese
3 cups hashed browns
1-1/2 cups frozen broccoli
1 cup cheese, grated (Cheddar or Monterey Jack)
1/2 cup mayonnaise
1/2 teaspoon dill
1 package crescent rolls
1 egg white

Preheat oven to 350 degrees. Place cream cheese, hash browns, broccoli, cheese, mayonnaise and dill in microwave-safe bowl. Microwave, stirring occasionally, until filling mixture is heated thoroughly. Place 2 crescents with short ends pressed together on parchment-lined baking sheet. One package of crescents will make 4 stuffed crescents. Place 1 large scoop of filling mixture in the center of each pair of crescents. Wrap the pointed end of each crescent around the mound of filling. This will help hold and seal the filling inside. There will be an opening on top. Brush the crescents with egg white. Bake for 10 to 15 minutes. Crescents should be golden brown.

Servings: 4

Presented by: Bass & Baskets Bed and Breakfast - Lake Ozark, Missouri

Did you know . . . dill has been around for thousands of years. It is mentioned in the Bible and in ancient Egyptian writings. The Greek and Roman cultures considered it a sign of fortuity, wealth and good luck. Dill was also honored by past cultures for its curative properties. Hippocrates, the "Father of Medicine," used dill as a means of cleaning one's mouth. Ancient soldiers applied burnt dill seeds to wounds to promote healing.

Personal touches . . .

_____
_____
_____
_____
_____
_____

helpful hints . . .

The trick to per-
fect crêpes is the
right pan - it
should be shallow
yet heavy with a
well-tempered
iron or non-stick
surface. It is very
important that
crêpe batter be
thin enough to
spread quickly; a
slight turn of the
wrist should be
enough to spread
batter evenly over
the bottom of the
pan. Crêpes can
be savory or sweet
and used for sim-
ple meals or for
special occasions.
Try experiment-
ing with your
own crêpe ideas!

*Personal
touches . . .*

_____

_____

_____

_____

_____

_____

Ruffled Crêpes Albemarle

Crêpes:
1-1/4 cups flour
2 tablespoons sugar
Pinch of salt
3 eggs
1-1/2 cups milk
2 tablespoons butter, melted

Egg Mixture:
7 eggs
1-1/2 cups milk
1/2 teaspoon salt
1/4 teaspoon pepper
1 tablespoon flour

Filling:
1 pound bacon, cooked and crumbled
2 cups Cheddar cheese, shredded

Garnish:
Chives
Roasted red pepper sauce (see page 90)

In a medium bowl, mix crêpe ingredients well and allow
mixture to sit for 15 minutes. Heat a non-stick crêpe pan.
Slightly brush pan with shortening to prime the first crêpe.
Proceed making the crêpes as in making pancakes. Peel off
the crêpe when it starts looking dry, and flip on to the other
side, which should cook in less time. Remove from pan,
and stack one finished crêpe atop another.

Preheat oven to 385 degrees and grease a standard muffin
tin. Combine egg mixture ingredients and set aside. Press
crêpes into tin, lightly ruffling the edges. Pour filling mixture into bottom of each crêpe. Carefully fill the rest of
each crêpe with egg mixture. Bake 15 to 20 minutes on
lowest oven rack. Egg mixture should be firm and crêpes
lightly browned. Serve 2 crêpes per individual serving
plate, garnished with red pepper sauce and chives.

Servings: 4

*Presented by: Albemarle Inn Bed & Breakfast -
Asheville, North Carolina*

Herbed Spinach Crêpes

Crêpes:
3 eggs
2 tablespoons flour
1 tablespoon milk
1 tablespoon water
1 tablespoon canola oil
1/2 teaspoon salt
Shortening to grease pan

Filling:
2 teaspoons canola oil
1/2 cup sweet Vidalia onion, sliced
2 cups fresh baby spinach leaves
1 teaspoon fresh thyme
Salt and pepper to season
6 ounces fresh feta cheese, grated

Did you know . . .
Vidalia onions are native to Vidalia, Georgia. They are exceptionally juicy and sweet. They are pale yellow and generally large in size. In regions where grown, they are available from May through June. Where availability is limited, Vidalia onions can also be purchased through mail order from other regions.

Place all crêpe ingredients in a blender, and blend for 2 minutes until well mixed. Heat a non-stick crêpe pan, preferably about 7 to 9 inches in diameter. Lightly brush pan with shortening to prime the first crêpes. Proceed making the crêpes as in making pancakes. This crêpe batter is thinner than pancake batter. Use less batter for each crêpe to produce soft and tender crêpes. Tilt the pan back and forth, spreading the batter toward the edges of the pan. Peel off the crêpe when it starts looking dry, and flip on to the other side, which should cook in less time. Remove from pan, and stack one finished crêpe atop another.

Using the same crêpe pan, heat the canola oil to high heat and sauté the onions until transparent, then add the spinach and fresh thyme together. Season with salt and pepper; set aside. This should be done quickly without burning the spinach. You want it just wilted and soft. When ready, assemble each crêpe by adding 2 tablespoons of filling onto half of the crêpe; filling with cheese. Plate and garnish.

Personal touches . . .

Servings: 6

Presented by: The Historic Inns of Abingdon, The Victoria & Albert Inn, The Love House Bed & Breakfast - Abingdon, Virginia

Did you know . . . scones are best when eaten the same day as prepared. They can be frozen and should be stored in a freezer-safe container or bag for up to two months. Reheat them in the oven or microwave.

Apricot and White Chocolate Scones

2/3 cup butter
3-1/4 cups flour
1/2 cup sugar
4 teaspoons baking powder
1/2 teaspoon salt
2/3 cup dried apricots or dates, finely chopped
1 cup white chocolate chips
2 eggs
2/3 cup half & half
Granulated sugar

Preheat oven to 400 degrees. Process butter, flour, sugar, baking powder and salt in a food processor until mixture is crumbly. Stir in apricots and white chocolate chips. By hand, add eggs and just enough half & half so dough forms a ball. Turn onto a floured surface and knead lightly 10 times. Roll dough out to 1/3-inch thickness. Using a biscuit cutter or a small juice glass (floured), cut into small round discs. Sprinkle with granulated sugar. Bake on a greased cooking sheet or parchment paper approximately 15 minutes or until golden in color. Serve warm.

Servings: 8

Presented by: Colby Hill Inn - Henniker, New Hampshire

Personal touches . . .

_____

_____

_____

_____

_____

_____

_____

Cream Tea Currant Scones

2 cups flour
1 tablespoon granulated sugar
2-1/2 teaspoons baking powder
1/4 teaspoon salt
4 tablespoons cold, unsalted butter
2 eggs
2/3 cup heavy cream
1/2 cup dried currants

In a small bowl, stir together flour, sugar, baking powder and salt. Cut in butter with a pastry blender. In a separate bowl, whisk together eggs and cream. Add all but 2 tablespoons of egg mixture to flour mixture. Stir in currants. Turn sticky dough onto floured surface. Knead gently 6 times. Form into 8-inch circle, slightly higher in the center. Cut into 8 sections. Brush with egg mixture. Bake 15 to 17 minutes, until golden brown. Serve with butter and lemon curd.

Servings: 8

Presented by: A La Provence Bed & Breakfast - Freeland, Washington

helpful hints . . .

It is best to use double-acting baking powder in scone recipes. Because baking soda should be replaced every six months, it is a good idea to test your baking soda for effectiveness. To do this, combine 1/2 cup hot water with 1 teaspoon baking powder. The mixture should bubble; if it does not, then it is no longer good.

Personal touches . . .

Did you know. . . scones made with cream are rich and cake-like in texture.

Plum and Almond Scones

1 cup almonds, flaked
2-1/4 cups all-purpose flour
1/2 cup sugar
2 teaspoons baking powder
1/2 teaspoon salt
1/2 stick (4 tablespoons) butter, cold
1 cup dried plums, roughly chopped
1 cup sour cream
1/2 cup cream or half & half
1 teaspoon almond essence

Heat a frying pan on medium heat and cook flaked almonds (dry) until golden brown. Remove from heat and cool. Sift together dry ingredients into a large mixing bowl. Rub in butter with a pastry blender until breadcrumb consistency is reached. Stir in plums and almonds. Add sour cream, cream or half & half and almond essence. Work together with a fork until a soft dough is formed. If dough is too dry, add a little more cream or half & half. Do not overwork the dough, or scones will be tough.

Personal touches . . .

_____

_____

_____

_____

_____

_____

_____

Spray a cookie sheet with non-stick cooking spray. Divide the dough into pieces that are approximately 3 ounces each, and rough shape into rounds. If you prefer, you can roll out the dough and use a round cutter. Place scones on sheet, brush with cream and bake at 400 degrees for 18 to 20 minutes, until lightly golden brown. Remove from oven and cool for 5 to 10 minutes. Serve while warm with butter and preserves, although they are delicious as is.

Servings: 8

Presented by: Henry Whipple House Bed & Breakfast - Bristol, New Hampshire

helpful hints . . .

Scones are easy to make and extremely time efficient. With little effort, you will be rewarded with delicious light and flaky scones. The most important thing to remember while making scones is to handle the dough as little as possible. Electric mixers are not recommended for use, as there is a tendency to overmix. Overmixing the dough will result in a heavy, dense and tough scone.

Personal touches . . .

Cocktails & Beginnings

beverages

Evergreen Inn Rum Punch

2 cups coconut rum
2 cups cran-raspberry juice
2 cups pineapple juice

Mix together and pour over an ice-filled pitcher. Serve in plastic glasses. Drink from a rocking chair facing west. Marvel at the sunset – vow to enjoy life's simplest pleasures.

Servings: 6 cups

Presented by: The Evergreen Inn Bed & Breakfast - Spring Lake, New Jersey

Did you know . . . rum is a type of liquor distilled from fermented molasses or sugarcane juice. The majority of the world's rum originates in the Caribbean. Slightly sweet, rum is used in a variety of cocktails such as daiquiris, piña coladas, mai tais and Cuba libres.

Personal touches . . .

_____
_____
_____
_____
_____
_____
_____

Did you know . . . the term "sangria" is derived from the Spanish word for "blood" and refers to the deep red color of the beverage. Sangria is typically made with red wine, fruit, fruit juices, soda water and liquor, brandy or cognac. "Sangria Blanco" is made with white wine instead of red wine but contains the same additional ingredients. Each are served cold over ice and are a refreshing summer treat.

Personal touches . . .

_____

_____

_____

_____

_____

_____

_____

Punch & Barbara's Sangria

1-1/2 to 2 cups (any) fresh fruit
Crystal Light® (any flavor) *
Ice cubes
Water
Seltzer water

Place fresh fruit in blender.   Add 1 tablespoon Crystal Light® and ice cubes to about 3/4 high in blender.   Pour enough water to cover all.   Pulse to crush ice.   This should be a slush consistency.   Pour mixture into pitcher.   Add seltzer to taste.

* 1 packet equals 1 tablespoon

Best Lemonade is made by cutting one half or whole lemon into quarters to use as fruit.   This can also become Barbara's Sangria by mixing with wine when serving.

Servings: 1 quart

Presented by: The John F. Craig House Bed & Breakfast - Cape May, New Jersey

Hot Cocoa Mix

1 (8-quart) box nonfat dry milk
1 – 6-ounce jar or 1-1/2 cups coffee mate
3 cups Nestlé® Quik® powder
1 cup powdered sugar

Combine all ingredients and mix well. Store in a sealed container. Mix will stay fresh for up to a year. For a delicious cup of hot chocolate, use 1/3 cup mixture with 1 cup hot milk. For a lighter taste, mix 1/3 cup mixture with 1 cup hot water. Top with freshly whipped cream and chocolate shavings.

Servings: 25 cups

Presented by: Blair-Moore House Bed & Breakfast - Jonesborough, Tennessee

Did you know... our founding fathers were fans of hot chocolate? In 1785, Thomas Jefferson wrote a letter to John Adams describing his esteem of drinking chocolate as a beverage and believed "the superiority of chocolate, both for health and nourishment, will soon give it the same preference over tea and coffee in America which it has in Spain."

The first recipe for a chocolate drink similar to hot cocoa was written in 1631 by Antonio Colmenero de Ledesma, an Andalusian physician, in a book focusing on the nature and quality of chocolate. The book was titled "Curioso Tratado de la Naturaleza y Calidad del Chocolate" which translated means "A Curious Treatise of the Nature and Quality of Chocolate." The following is a description of the ingredients included in the chocolate drink recipe:

"Take one hundred cocoa beans, two chilies, a handful of anise seed and two vanilla (two pulverized Alexandria roses can be substituted), two drams of cinnamon, one dozen almonds and the same amount of hazelnuts, half a pound of white sugar and enough annatto to give some color. And there you have the king of chocolates."

Personal touches . . .

_____

_____

_____

_____

_____

_____

_____

soups & salads

Cold Raspberry Soup

2 – 16-ounce bags of frozen raspberries
4 cups cran-raspberry juice
3/4 cup sugar
1-1/2 teaspoons ground cinnamon
1/2 teaspoon ground clove
2 tablespoons lemon juice
1 – 32-ounce container raspberry flavored yogurt
1/2 cup fat free vanilla yogurt

In a blender, purée raspberries and 2 cups cran-raspberry juice. Transfer to a large sauce pan and add remainder of cran-raspberry juice, sugar, cinnamon and cloves. Bring just to a boil over medium heat. Remove from heat and strain to remove seeds. Allow to cool. Whisk in lemon juice and raspberry yogurt. Refrigerate until cold. To serve, pour into small bowls and top with a dollop of vanilla yogurt.

Servings: 8 to 12

Presented by: Aberdeen Mansion Bed and Breakfast - Aberdeen, Washington

Personal touches . . .

_____

_____

_____

_____

_____

_____

_____

helpful hints . . .

Raspberries are regarded as one of the most strongly flavored members of the berry family. When choosing raspberries, look for those that are bright in color and without a hull. Those that still contain a hull were picked too soon and will inevitably be tart. Soft, shriveled or molded berries should be discarded. Raspberries should be stored in the refrigerator, single layered in a moisture proof container. They will remain consumable for two to three days.

Tropical Fruit Salad

1/2 cup sugar
1/2 cup water
1 small pineapple
2 medium mangos
3 kiwis
1 small papaya
Berries in season (raspberries, blueberries or strawberries)
1/4 cup Grand Marnier®
Squeeze of lime or lemon
2 passion fruits

Garnish and Accompaniments:
Whipped cream, crème fraîche or ice cream
Fresh mint sprigs

Heat the sugar and water over low heat until the sugar dissolves. Bring to a boil and simmer about two minutes. Pour the syrup into a medium bowl and let cool. Cut the pineapple, mangos, kiwis and papaya in equal sized chunks. Add the berries, if desired, for a nice variety in taste and color. Add the Grand Marnier® and squeeze of lemon or lime. Pour the cooled syrup over the fruit and cover with plastic wrap. Allow to marinate in the refrigerator for at least 3 hours and up to 12 hours.

Slice open the passion fruits and scoop the seeds into a bowl. Gently spoon the fruit mixture into chilled dessert bowls or parfait glasses and sprinkle with passion fruit seeds. You may also top this with freshly whipped cream, crème fraîche or ice cream. Garnish with mint and serve.

Servings: 4

Presented by: Blair-Moore House Bed & Breakfast - Jonesborough, Tennessee

Personal touches . . .

_____

_____

_____

_____

_____

_____

_____

Did you know . . .
Eagle Brand® was created by Gail Borden in 1856 in an effort to provide milk that would remain safe and wholesome for consumption. At the time, lack of refrigeration and preservation techniques resulted in high infant mortality rates. Borden's discovery is credited for significantly lowering these rates. It was also utilized during the Civil War by military personnel in need of safe nutritional nourishment found in preserved milk.

Personal touches . . .

_____

_____

_____

_____

_____

_____

Luncheon Noodle Salad

1 pound multi-colored curly noodles
3 carrots, grated or chopped
2 green peppers, chopped
1 onion, diced
2 cups mayonnaise
1 cup white vinegar
3/4 cup white sugar
1 can Eagle Brand® condensed milk (not evaporated)

Cook and the drain the noodles and allow to cool. Add vegetables to noodles. In a separate bowl, combine mayonnaise, vinegar, sugar and condensed milk. Combine sauce with noodles and vegetables until well mixed. Refrigerate well before serving.

Servings: 4

Presented by: Alaska Gold Rush Bed & Breakfast Inn - Palmer, Alaska

Blair-Moore House Chicken Salad

1 cup green grapes, halved or quartered
1 cup Hellman's® mayonnaise or homemade mayonnaise
1 tablespoon fresh lemon juice
Salt to taste
Freshly ground pepper to taste
4 cups cooked chicken breast, chopped
1 cup pecan or almonds, toasted and chopped or sliced

Mix grapes, mayonnaise, lemon juice, salt and pepper and then gently add the chicken and toasted nuts. May be served on lettuce leaves or on thickly sliced nine grain bread.

Presented by: The Blair-Moore House Bed & Breakfast - Jonesborough, Tennessee

helpful hints . . .

When purchasing fresh grapes, look for fruit that is fully colored, plump and firmly attached to stems. White or green grapes should have a pale hue of yellow. Dark grapes should be deeply colored with no sign of green. Store grapes in the refrigerator unwashed and in a plastic bag. In general, grapes will keep for up to a week but as time passes their quality will lessen. Because grapes are sprayed with insecticide, you should thoroughly wash them before they are consumed or used. Fresh grapes are best when removed from the refrigerator at least thirty minutes before serving.

Personal touches . . .

Sauerkraut Soup

1-3/4 pounds Morse's® Sauerkraut*
9-1/2 cups vegetable stock
3 large onions, roughly chopped
2 to 3 cloves garlic, finely chopped
Olive oil
3 medium potatoes, grated
1/2 teaspoon fennel seeds
1/2 teaspoon caraway seeds
1 teaspoon paprika
1/2 teaspoon salt
Fresh ground pepper to taste
1 can tomatoes
2 medium sized carrots, thinly sliced
1 package Melissa's® Soyrizo
　　(For those who are meat eaters, we use chorizo.)

Drain the sauerkraut, chop roughly and simmer in vegetable stock for 30 minutes. Vegetable bouillon cubes, 1 cube to 1 cup of water, or a vegetable broth can be substituted for vegetable stock. While simmering sauerkraut, sauté onions and garlic in a generous amount of olive oil until transparent.

*Personal
touches . . .*

_____

_____

_____

_____

_____

_____

Grate the potatoes, with peel, and place in cold water to keep fresh. Add the onions, garlic, drained potatoes, fennel, caraway, paprika, salt, pepper, tomatoes and carrots to the sauerkraut mixture. Cover and boil gently for 30 minutes longer. About 20 minutes into the last step, throw the Soyrizo in the mixture and stir vigorously. Serve hot with dark bread and butter. Freezes well.

*Morse's® Sauerkraut is produced locally in Waldoboro, Maine, but is shipped nationwide.

Servings: 6 to 8

Presented by: The Roaring Lion Bed and Breakfast - Waldoboro, Maine

Did you know . . . sauerkraut is a German term meaning "sour cabbage." It is oftentimes assumed to be of German descent. In actuality, while building the Great Wall of China over 2,000 years ago, Chinese laborers are recorded to have eaten it as a regular staple of their diets. Sauerkraut is a combination of shredded cabbage, salt and spices, which are allowed to ferment. Remember to rinse sauerkraut before using it and enjoy as an accompaniment to sandwiches, casseroles, as a side dish and in soups.

Personal touches . . .

_____

_____

_____

_____

_____

_____

_____

dips, spreads & sauces

Fresh Vegetable Salsa

2 cups red plum tomatoes, diced
2 cups yellow tomatoes, diced
   (substitute red if yellow is not available)
2 cups orange tomatoes
   (substitute red if orange is not available)
1 small red onion
1/4 cup yellow pepper, diced
   (substitute green if yellow is not available)
1/4 cup red pepper, diced
   (substitute green if red is not available)
1/4 cup orange pepper, diced
   (substitute green if orange is not available)
1/4 cup green pepper, diced
1/2 cup zucchini, diced
1/2 teaspoon garlic, minced
2 tablespoons lemon juice
2 teaspoons apple cider vinegar
1 teaspoon dried Italian herb seasoning
1 teaspoon seasoning salt
1/2 teaspoon sugar
Fresh ground pepper and salt to taste
1/4 cup cilantro, chopped

*Personal
touches . . .*

_____

_____

_____

_____

_____

_____

Dice all vegetables into 1/4-inch pieces. Place in a bowl, mix lightly and set aside. In a small bowl, mix garlic, lemon juice, apple cider vinegar, Italian herb seasoning, seasoning salt, sugar, pepper and salt. Pour over vegetables. Add cilantro and mix well. Let sit at room temperature 30 to 45 minutes or 3 hours in refrigerator. Stir every 15 to 30 minutes.

Servings: 8 cups

Presented by: Forgett-Me-Nott Bed & Breakfast - Victoria, British Columbia

Personal touches . . .

_____

_____

_____

_____

_____

_____

_____

Did you know . . . cumin is a caraway seed shaped spice that dates back to the Old Testament. It is the dried fruit of a plant in the parsley family. As with all seeds, herbs and spices, it should be stored in a cool, dark place for no more than 6 months.

Roasted Red Pepper Sauce

1 – 16-ounce jar roasted sweet red peppers
1 teaspoon onion powder
1 tablespoon extra virgin olive oil
1 teaspoon lemon juice, or to taste
2 tablespoons vegetable stock (more for thinner sauce)
1/2 teaspoon ground cumin
Salt to taste
Fresh ground pepper to taste

Combine all ingredients in a blender and process until smooth and creamy.

Servings: 1-1/2 cups

Presented by: Albemarle Inn Bed & Breakfast - Asheville, North Carolina

Personal touches . . .

Bleu Cheese Walnut Spread

8 ounces cream cheese, softened
3 ounces bleu cheese
1 tablespoon dry sherry or wine
1/2 cup walnuts, chopped
2 tablespoons parsley, minced
1/8 teaspoon garlic powder
1 tablespoon horseradish
Cayenne pepper sauce to taste

In food processor, blend cheeses and sherry to a creamy texture. Add remaining ingredients and process just until blended. The walnuts should still be in good sized pieces, not flakes. If softer mixture is desired, thin with sour cream. Serve with crackers, cucumbers, celery, shrimp or apple slices. Store covered in refrigerator up to 2 weeks.

Servings: 3 to 4

Presented by: The John F. Craig House Bed & Breakfast - Cape May, New Jersey

Did you know . . . when cooking with cayenne pepper and cayenne pepper sauces, it is a good idea to remember that a little bit goes a long way! Add just a dash or two in recipes for 2 to 4 servings. Taste test the recipe, and increase dash by dash until the dish has reached desired heat level. It is better to be safe then sorry!

Personal touches . . .

Setting the Table

Use the above illustration as a guide for properly setting your table. The illustration is for a meal that will consist of a beverage, soup, salad and main entrée, and dessert and coffee following the main course.

Glasses and Cups

※ Water glasses are always placed above the dinner knife, and all other drinking glasses are arranged around the water glass. Coffee cups, tea cups and saucers can placed to the right of the knife and spoon.

Bowls and Plates

※ Soup bowls are always placed on top of the dinner plate.

※ Salad plates are placed just above and slightly to the left of forks.

※ Dinner plates should be placed 2 inches from the table's edge. If you are using placemats, dinner plates should be centered on the placemat. If you are not using placemats, dinner plates should be centered squarely in front of each chair.

※ Bread plates are always placed above and slightly to the right of the salad plate.

※ Many hosts prefer to serve meals in multiple courses. During this process, only one dish from the original place setting will be used and then removed and replaced by the following course. For example, if soup is the first served course, the soup bowl will be placed on top of the dinner plate. When the soup bowl is removed it will then be replaced with the salad dish.

Silverware

※ Silverware is always placed on the table in the order that it will be used, and you should never place more silverware on the table than will be used during the meal.

※ Forks are always placed on the left side of the dinner plate, while spoons and knives are placed on the right side. The knife should be placed closest to the plate with the blade facing inward and the spoon to the right of the knife. Butter knives are always laid flat on the bread plate.

※ Dessert silverware should be centered parallel above the dinner plate.

Napkins & Place Cards

※ Napkins are placed on the table, to the inside of drinking glasses or to the left of forks.

※ Place cards are a great idea for large dinner parties and should be placed to the left of drinking glasses above the dessert utensils.

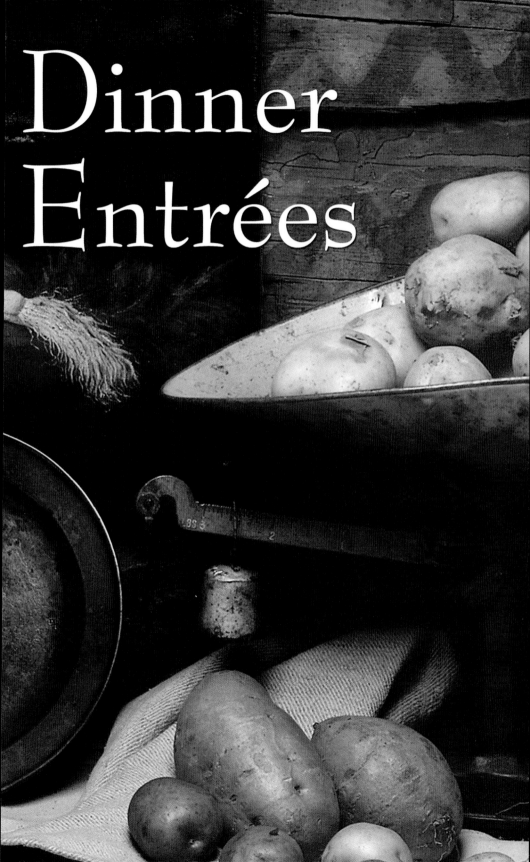

Dinner
Entrées

beef, pork & lamb

Barbeque Meatballs

Meatballs:
3 pounds ground beef
2 cups rolled oats
12 ounces evaporated milk
1 cup onion, chopped
2 eggs
1 teaspoon salt
1/2 teaspoon pepper
1/2 teaspoon garlic powder

Sauce:
2 cups ketchup
1-1/2 cups brown sugar
1/2 teaspoon garlic powder
2 tablespoons liquid smoke
1/2 cup onion, finely chopped
1/2 cup water – if sauce is too thick to pour

Preheat oven to 350 degrees. Combine meatball ingredients and mix well. Shape into small balls. Place a single layer on greased baking pans. Combine all sauce ingredients and mix well. Spoon sauce over meatballs. Bake for 1 hour. May be frozen and reheated.

Servings: 60 to 100 meatballs

Presented by: Alaska Gold Rush Bed & Breakfast Inn - Palmer, Alaska

Did you know . . . ketchup is thought to have originated from a 17th century Chinese type of fermented fish sauce and condiment known as ke-tsiap.

Personal touches . . .

_____
_____
_____
_____
_____
_____
_____

Did you know . . .
Beef Burgundy, also
known as Boeuf (à
la) Bourguignon, is a
French term for a
beef stew made 'in
the style of
Burgundy,' or
Burgundian beef. It
is customarily made
with a red Burgundy
wine as part of the
liquid, and usually
onions and
mushrooms. It can
also be made with
white Burgundy, and
often a small amount
of brandy is added to
the stew as well.

Boeuf Bourguignon (Beef Burgundy)

3 pounds lean chuck fillet, cut in 1-inch cubes
   and dried on paper towels
10 cloves garlic, sliced (5 or 6 slices per clove)
2 bunches fresh rosemary, lightly pounded
2 medium sprigs thyme
1-1/2 teaspoons fresh thyme, finely chopped
4 cups burgundy wine, more if needed
2 tablespoons butter, more if needed
2 tablespoons extra virgin olive oil, more if needed
6 slices thick bacon, diced
3 tablespoons flour
2 teaspoons salt
1 teaspoon fresh ground black pepper
2 bay leaves
1 to 2 cups beef stock
12 small white pearl onions
12 small red pearl onions
1-1/2 pounds small, 1/2-inch to 3/4-inch mushrooms,
   stems trimmed
3 tablespoons butter

In a large bowl, place beef cubes, garlic, rosemary and thyme, and cover with wine. Refrigerate overnight. The next day, remove beef cubes from the marinade, squeeze cubes to remove as much of the marinade as possible and air dry for at least 2 hours while reserving the marinade.

Preheat oven to 425 degrees. In a heavy skillet, heat butter and oil. Place bacon in skillet and cook until lightly browned; move with slotted spoon to a heavy, lidded casserole dish. In the same skillet, brown the beef a few pieces at a time on all sides, adding more oil if necessary. Place beef cubes in casserole dish as they complete browning. Place dish over a top burner and bring to a very low heat. Sprinkle flour on the beef cubes, toss gently, and cook until flour is absorbed. Remove dish cover and place in the oven. Cook 4 to 5 minutes, then toss meat and cook 5 minutes more to totally sear the meat.

Personal
touches . . .

_____

_____

_____

_____

_____

_____

_____

Reduce oven temperature to 325 degrees. Return the dish to the top of stove and pour in the reserved wine marinade, salt, pepper, bay leaves and 1/2 of the beef stock. Bring to a simmer and then cover. Place covered dish in oven and cook for 1-1/2 to 2 hours or until meat is almost tender. Check frequently to make sure that liquid has not boiled away. Add more burgundy and beef stock as necessary.

Peel the pearl onions and cut a large "X" in the root end to eliminate separation. Clean and dry the small mushrooms, keeping the trimmed stems in place. Lightly sauté the onions and mushrooms in butter. Sprinkle with salt and pepper. Add the onions and mushrooms to the stew and cook 30 to 45 minutes longer, or until meat and vegetables are tender. Check frequently to make sure that liquid has not boiled. Serve in large bowls with fresh hot French bread.

Servings: 4

Presented by: The Wyman Hotel & Inn - Silverton, Colorado

Personal touches . . .

_____

_____

_____

_____

_____

_____

_____

*Did you know . . .
gremolata, also
spelled gremolada,
is a garnish usually
made of minced
parsley, lemon peel
and garlic. It is
typically sprinkled
over osso buco (an
Italian veal shank
dish) and other
dishes, adding a
fresh, sprightly
flavor.*

Lamb Shank with Gremolata Sauce

Lamb Shanks:
4 lamb shanks (14 to 16 ounces)*
Salt to taste
Pepper to taste
1/4 cup flour
2 tablespoons olive oil
2 tablespoons unsalted butter
1 large carrot, finely chopped
1 stalk celery, finely chopped
2 medium onions, diced
2 garlic cloves, minced
1 cup white wine
1 cup chicken broth
1 can (28 ounces) plum tomatoes, chopped
1/2 cup black kalamata olives, pitted and chopped
1 teaspoon fresh rosemary
1 teaspoon fresh parsley
1 bay leaf

Gremolata:
3 tablespoons fresh parsley, minced
1 tablespoon orange zest, grated
1 teaspoon lemon zest, grated
1 clove garlic, finely minced
1/2 cup red wine
Salt and pepper

*Pork or veal shanks and osso buco (an Italian veal shank
dish) can be substituted.

*Personal
touches . . .*

_____

_____

_____

_____

_____

_____

_____

Pat shanks dry, season with salt and pepper and lightly coat with the flour. Heat oil and butter in oven-proof pot over high heat and brown the shanks for 10 to 12 minutes; remove and transfer to a plate. Reduce the heat and add the carrot, celery, onions and garlic for 4 to 5 minutes. Add the remaining ingredients; bring to a boil and stir-scrape all the goodness from the bottom of the pan. Add the shanks to the pot in one layer (if you don't have a large enough pot, use a deep lasagna pan). Cover and place in oven at 325 degrees for approximately 2-1/2 hours until tender. Just before removing the shanks from the oven, mix the gremolata ingredients in a large saucepan until heated, for 4 to 5 minutes. Remove the shanks from the pan and take the rest of the pan ingredients (except for the bay leaf), stir together with the gremolata and top the shanks with this sauce. Perfect served over garlic mashed potatoes.

Servings: 4

Presented by: Beal House Inn and Restaurant - Littleton, New Hampshire

Personal touches . . .

_____

_____

_____

_____

_____

_____

_____

helpful hints . . .

Fine sea salt is best stored in a tightly sealed glass jar. A few grains of brown rice in the shaker help to absorb moisture, keeping the salt flowing.

Pork Tenderloin with Caramelized Balsamic Onions

2 – 1 to 1-1/2 pound pork tenderloins
3 large Bermuda onions, halved and very thinly sliced
2 tablespoons butter
2 tablespoons olive oil
3 tablespoons balsamic vinegar
3 tablespoons dark brown sugar
1/4 teaspoon sea salt
1/4 teaspoon fresh ground black pepper
1 tablespoon extra virgin olive oil

Wash tenderloin, paper towel dry and set out at room temperature for about 1 hour to dry. Warm a heavy skillet or wok over medium high heat, and caramelize the onions in the butter and olive oil until light brown. Add vinegar and brown sugar, increase heat to high and stir for 2 minutes. Remove from heat and add salt and pepper. Rub tenderloin with virgin olive oil and let set for 10 minutes.

Preheat oven to 375 degrees. Warm a heavy skillet over high heat and lightly sear the tenderloins on all sides. Place tenderloin in oil-covered roasting pan; place onion mixture over tenderloins and roast until internal temperature is 145 degrees. Remove from oven and keep covered for at least 5 minutes. Carve across the grain about 3/4-inch thick, and drizzle onion and juices over tenderloin slices.

Servings: 6

Presented by: The Wyman Hotel and Inn - Silverton, Colorado

Personal touches . . .

_____

_____

_____

_____

_____

_____

_____

Bedouin Lamb

1/4 cup soy sauce
1/4 cup extra virgin olive oil
1/4 cup dry red wine
2 tablespoons lime juice
3 tablespoons fresh rosemary
1 teaspoon dark brown sugar
1-1/2 pounds lean, boneless lamb, cut into 1-inch cubes

In a large stainless steel bowl, combine the soy sauce, oil, wine, lime juice, rosemary and brown sugar. Blend well and add the lamb, stirring to coat evenly. Refrigerate for at least 6 to 8 hours, stirring occasionally to keep the meat coated. Remove the lamb from the marinade and pat dry with paper towels. Reserve the marinade. Thread the lamb cubes on long metal skewers and cook on a preheated, well-oiled grill for about 15 minutes, turning frequently, and brush with the reserved marinade. Serve on a bed of rice with slivered almonds and walnuts.

For an interesting change of flavor, skewer onion sections and Key or Persian limes between the lamb cubes. Fresh, long stemmed rosemary can be used in place of the metal skewers; reduce the rosemary in marinade by 2 table-spoons.

Servings: 4

Presented by: The Wyman Hotel & Inn - Silverton, Colorado

Personal touches . . .

poultry, fish & shrimp

Rosemary Garlic Shrimp with Penne

1 pound frozen, pre-cooked shrimp
3 tablespoons butter
2 tablespoons Italian seasoning blend
1 tablespoon garlic powder
1 pound penne pasta or pasta of choice
3 tablespoons olive oil
2 tablespoons rosemary garlic seasoning such as Tone's®
1 cup four cheese blend, grated or shredded

Remove tails from shrimp. Melt 2 tablespoons butter over medium heat in a 10-inch or 12-inch skillet. Sauté shrimp with butter, Italian seasonings and garlic powder. In the meantime, begin to cook pasta to desired firmness. Once shrimp is heated through, move to a separate bowl, leaving liquids in pan. Add remaining 1 tablespoon butter, olive oil and rosemary garlic seasoning, and stir until warm. Put the shrimp back in the pan; stir to coat. Sprinkle with cheese and serve warm with penne.

Servings: 4 to 6

Presented by: The Painted Lady Bed and Breakfast - Elmira, New York

Personal touches . . .

Game Hens with Orange Jus and Sautéed Tomato Halves

2 game hens (Guinea fowl), 2 to 2-1/2 pounds each,
   rinsed and paper towel dried
Sea salt to taste
White pepper, freshly ground to taste
6 oranges, rinsed, cut in half
2 fresh rosemary sprigs
Ordinary household string
5 tablespoons unsalted butter
4 medium leeks, white and tender parts,
   wash well and cross cut into 1-inch pieces
1/2 cup shallots, peeled and roughly chopped
3 juniper berries, crushed
2 bay leaves
1 tablespoon white peppercorns
2 cups orange juice, freshly squeezed
1/4 cup dry white wine
1-1/2 pounds Roma tomatoes, halved

Preheat oven to 400 degrees. Season hens inside and out with salt and pepper, and place half of orange with a sprig of rosemary into the cavity of each hen. Tie legs of each hen together with ordinary household string. Heat 3 tablespoons of butter in a large deep skillet over medium heat. When butter is melted and foamy, place the hens breast down in skillet, turn to brown evenly on all sides. Remove hens from skillet and place in a medium roasting pan. Brush completely with melted butter, place in oven and roast 30 minutes, basting every 10 minutes with pan juices.

continued on page 106

Did you know . . . juniper berries are blue-black in color and very pungent, making them too bitter to eat raw. They are commonly dried and crushed and used to flavor meats and sauces. Juniper berries are also used as the characteristic flavoring of gin.

Personal touches . . .

continued from page 105

Meanwhile, peel remaining oranges with a sharp knife, removing all the bitter white pith over a medium bowl to catch the juices. Cut in between membranes to release orange segments and set aside. Melt 1 tablespoon of butter in a large skillet over medium high heat; add half of orange segments, leeks, shallots, berries, bay leaves and peppercorns. Sauté 2 to 3 minutes, add 2 cups of orange juice and cook on medium heat 5 minutes. Season with salt and pepper.

Reduce heat to 370 degrees. Turn hens and roast 20 minutes. Add vegetables and baste hens often during roasting for 30 or more minutes, or until juices run clear. Transfer hens to a warmed large platter, cover with foil and keep warm. Strain vegetables and pan juices into a small saucepan, discarding vegetables. Add remaining cup of orange juice and wine and cook over moderately high heat, about 3 to 5 minutes. Keep warm.

Heat remaining tablespoon of butter in a medium skillet over medium high heat, and add tomatoes, cut side down. Sprinkle them lightly with salt and pepper and sauté with remaining orange segments for 1 to 2 minutes, turning once. Keep warm.

At this point, the hens need to be carved into 4 servings. The following two methods can be used to appropriately carve the hens for serving.

Method 1: Remove and discard string from legs. Cut away legs and thighs with a sharp knife, slicing nearest to the breast cavity – slightly twisting leg to expose and more easily disjoint thigh from breast cavity. Repeat process for wings. Resting hen on its side or on its back, slice between breast cavity and flesh to remove half breast in one piece. Repeat process.

Personal touches . . .

_____

_____

_____

_____

_____

_____

Method 2: With poultry shears, cut around and remove the wishbone, cut through the center of breastbone toward rear. Repeat cutting process through the center of the backbone, or make the cut on each side of the backbone and discard.

Once you have carved the hens, arrange half of a hen, cut side down, on pre-warmed dinner plates. Spoon tomato-orange mixture alongside hen, pour orange jus over each serving and serve remaining jus from a sauceboat kept warm at the table. Enjoy with accompaniments such as basmati rice, tiny potato dumplings or couscous, and with your favorite white wine – perhaps a dry Riesling, crispy Chardonnay or Sauvignon Blanc.

Note: If a thermometer is not available to check doneness, insert a carving fork into hen cavity and allow juices to drain. If juices run clear, hens are done. If juices have a pink tinge, roast hens another 5 to 10 minutes and test again for doneness.

Servings: 4

Presented by: A Touch of Europe® Bed & Breakfast and Fine Dining - Yakima, Washington

Personal touches . . .

_____

_____

_____

_____

_____

_____

_____

*Did you know . . .
snapper is available
fresh all year with a
peak season during
the summer. The best
aspect about cooking
with snapper is that
it is suitable for
virtually any cooking
method. The most
common size
available is between
2 and 8 pounds,
although they can
grow up to 35
pounds. The smaller
sizes are usually sold
whole, while the
larger sizes are sold
in steaks and filets.*

Snapper Tropical

1/4 cup vegetable oil
4 snapper filets (8 ounces each)
4 tablespoons flour
1/2 cup fish or chicken stock, unsalted
1/2 cup dark rum
4 fresh basil leaves, chopped
1/2 cup orange juice
1 tablespoon butter
2 cups diced fresh fruit such as bananas,
    oranges and/or strawberries
Salt and pepper to taste

Preheat oven to 350 degrees. Heat the vegetable oil in a pan while you lightly dredge the snapper in the flour and shake off all excess. Sauté both sides of the snapper filets in the oil until lightly browned, then discard the vegetable oil. Deglaze the pan with the fish stock and rum, and let reduce for 2 to 3 minutes. Add the basil, orange juice and butter to thicken the sauce. Add the fresh fruit, salt and pepper, and place in the oven for a final 4 to 5 minutes of cooking. Plate the fish and top with the fresh fruit sauce.

For variety, use seasonal fruit combinations such as kiwi, mango, papaya, pear, apple, grape or peach.

Servings: 4

Presented by: Beal House Inn and Restaurant - Littleton, New Hampshire

*Personal
touches . . .*

Shrimp Creole

1 medium onion, minced
2 tablespoons butter, margarine or oil
1 cup green pepper, chopped
1 cup celery, diced
1 bay leaf, crushed
1 teaspoon parsley, snipped
1/8 teaspoon cayenne red pepper
1 can tomato paste
1 to 2 cups water
2 cups fresh or frozen shrimp, cleaned and cooked
3 cups hot cooked rice

Cook and stir onion in butter or oil until tender. Stir in remaining ingredients except shrimp and rice. Cook over low heat, stirring occasionally for about 30 minutes. Stir in shrimp. Heat through and serve over rice.

Servings: 6

Presented by: Mill Creek Homestead Bed & Breakfast - Bird-in-Hand, Pennsylvania

helpful hints . . .

The most famous and popular dish of Creole heritage is gumbo. Creole cookery reflects the full-flavored combination of the best of French, Spanish and African cuisines. It encompasses a cooking style that emphasizes butter and cream, creating a more sophisticated result than Cajun cooking, which emphasizes the use of large amounts of pork fat. Creole cooking uses more tomatoes while the Cajun style uses more spices. Both cuisines rely on the culinary "holy trinity" of chopped green peppers, onions and celery.

Personal touches . . .

_____
_____
_____
_____
_____
_____

Herbed Poached Salmon

Salmon:
2 cups mixed fresh herbs, combination of thyme,
   oregano, basil, sage and parsley, wrapped in
   cheesecloth and tied with twine as a bouquet garni
2 gallons of tepid water
2 tablespoons whole peppercorns
2 lemons cut in wedges
1 – 10-pound fresh Atlantic salmon
3 cups white wine

Herb Mayonnaise:
4 cups mayonnaise
1 cup chopped, mixed fresh herbs, combination of dill,
   parsley, thyme, oregano and basil
Juice of two lemons
Salt and pepper

Garnish:
2 English cucumbers, scored and sliced across
Orange crowns
2 stuffed green olives
Kale
Bright berries to contrast the orange crowns

Salmon
You will need 1/2 of a yard of cheesecloth, kitchen twine
and a 30-inch poaching pan to prepare the salmon. Set
poaching pan on stovetop. Cover the two largest eyes of
the range. Add torn herbs, water, peppercorns and lemon
wedges. Bring to a simmering point. Rinse the whole
salmon, washing cavity and head. Keep gills and head
intact. Spread the cheesecloth open on top of a large chop-
ping board or clean countertop. Lay the fish across the
cloth, following the longest dimension to cover the full
length of the salmon. Wrap the salmon carefully, doubling
over to cover every part of the fish. String and tie with
knots around the poaching pan, making sure that liquid
covers the entire length and thickness of the fish. Pour the
white wine over fish and poach 30 to 45 minutes. Salmon

*Personal
touches . . .*

_____

_____

_____

_____

_____

_____

is cooked when the thickest part of the fish flesh bounces back without any impression. Remove the pan and leave fish to cool in the court bouillon. When cooked, remove from liquid and cool overnight in refrigerator. The fish stock can be saved and used for making Cioppino or any other type of fish soup. The next day, open the wrapping carefully with sharp scissors, and discard twines and cheesecloth. Set the cold fish on a board and continue removing the skin and dark linings underneath the skin. Do both sides without ruining the flesh and the shape of the fish.

Herb Mayonnaise
Blend all the mayonnaise ingredients in a medium-sized mixing bowl using a rubber spatula. Transfer the whole fish carefully onto a serving tray and cover the first side with half of the herb mayonnaise. Reserve the other half to serve as extra dressing on the table. Cover the head as well, leaving the eyes uncovered.

Garnish
After covering one side of the fish entirely with the herbed mayonnaise, start shingling the fish body with the thin slices of cucumber, trying to simulate scales. You may leave off the face area, just adding a cross slice of stuffed green olives for the eye. Finish presentation with kale, surrounding the fish, and accent with fruit or vegetable garnishes.

"I serve this as a centerpiece at my inns for receptions and special events. If there is someone manning the buffet table, this person is usually in charge of serving this dish, making sure that the flesh underneath the salmon vertebra is also served with enough mayonnaise and cumber slices. I use this as one of my catering signatures. This is a winner!" –Innkeeper Hazel Ramos-Cano

Servings: 4 to 6

Presented by: The Historic Inns of Abingdon: Victoria & Albert Inn, The Love House Bed & Breakfast - Abingdon, Virginia

Did you know . . .
bouquet garni is a cooking term for a bundle of herbs that have been tied together or placed in cheesecloth in order to "tie" or "bag" herbs, enabling easy removal before a dish is served. Bouquet garni is commonly used to flavor broths, soups and stews. The most frequently used herb combination for bouquet garni is bay leaf, parsley and thyme.

Personal touches . . .

_____

_____

_____

_____

_____

_____

Did you know . . .
cod is a popular
saltwater fish that is
native to the Pacific
and North Atlantic
Oceans. They can
weigh from 1-1/2 to
100 pounds. Cod is
popular for its white,
lean and very firm
mild-flavored meat.
Cod is available year-
round and can be
baked, braised,
broiled, fried and
poached.

Filet of Pacific Wild Cod with Red Onion Confit and Bruised Spinach

1-1/2 pounds cod filet, cut into four portions
  (prepared in advance)
2-1/2 ounces (about) coarse sea salt
4 tablespoons lime juice, freshly squeezed
2 tablespoons olive oil
2 cups red onions, half moon sliced,
  each about 1/8- to 1/4-inch thick
Fine sea salt to taste
White pepper, freshly ground to taste
1/4 cup orange juice, freshly squeezed
Pinch of sugar
Mélange peppercorns, coarsely ground to taste
4 tablespoons unsalted butter
3 cups baby spinach leaves, loosely packed
4 tablespoons unsalted butter

Garnish:
Tomato wedges
Lemon slices

Rinse cod, pat dry with paper towels and place in a shallow glass dish. Sprinkle with coarse sea salt and lime juice. Cover with plastic wrap and refrigerate 24 hours. Due to the delicacy of cod, the best manner to prepare this dish is to pre-assemble and pre-measure recipe ingredients. This recipe begins the cooking process with ingredients that require longer cooking times and can be prepared ahead of time and set aside.

To cook onions, heat a large skillet over medium high heat for 1 minute. Pour in olive oil and swirl to coat pan. As soon as oil is simmering, but not smoking, add onions in an even layer, and then sprinkle lightly with fine sea salt and pepper, letting them cook undisturbed until they begin to soften, about 2 to 3 minutes. Turn heat to medium, add orange juice and sugar. Cook 20 to 30 more minutes or until onions are very soft and slightly thickened. Season

Personal
touches . . .

_____

_____

_____

_____

_____

_____

again with fine sea salt and white pepper if needed and remove onions with a slotted spoon; discard oil. Place cooked onions in a warm shallow dish, cover and keep warm, reheat if necessary, but do not cook.

Remove cod from refrigerator, pat dry with paper towels and sprinkle with mélange pepper. Heat 2 tablespoons of butter in a large non-stick skillet over medium high heat. Cook one side of cod until nicely colored – turn over and cook until golden brown and opaque in the center, about 2 minutes per side. Place a filet in the center of each pre-warmed dinner plate, spoon some pan drippings over each serving, cover with foil to keep warm.

Using the same skillet, turn heat to high and add 2 table-spoons butter. Pinch spinach to bruise, and toss leaves in the skillet. Turn off heat; again toss spinach and sprinkle lightly with salt and pepper. Remove spinach from the skillet and arrange it alongside each filet. Spoon warm confit over each filet and garnish with tomato wedges and lemon slices.

Enjoy with a glass of your favorite Semillon, Pinot Gris, Sauvignon Blanc or perhaps a Viognier.

Servings: 4

Presented by: A Touch of Europe® Bed & Breakfast and Fine Dining - Yakima, Washington

Personal touches . . .

_____

_____

_____

_____

_____

_____

Did you know . . . raw shrimp should smell of the sea with no hint of ammonia. Cooked, shelled shrimp should look plump and succulent. Whether or not to devein shrimp is a matter of personal preference. In general, small and medium shrimp do not need deveining except for cosmetic purposes. However, because the intestinal vein of larger shrimp contains grit, it should be removed. Shrimp can be prepared in a variety of ways including boiling, frying and grilling.

Personal touches . . .

_____

_____

_____

_____

_____

_____

Shrimp and Scallop Chipotle

Shrimp:
4 tablespoons olive oil
8 large shrimps
12 sea scallops

Chipotle Butter:
1/2 cup unsalted butter, softened
1-1/2 teaspoons seeded chipotle (adobo) chilies,
    finely minced – also found canned
1/4 teaspoon salt
1 tablespoon your favorite hot sauce

Cornmeal Pancakes:
3 tablespoons vegetable oil
1 cup flour
1/2 cup fine yellow cornmeal
    (or for variety use red or blue cornmeal)
1/4 teaspoon baking powder
1/4 teaspoon baking soda
1/4 teaspoon sugar
1/4 teaspoon salt
1 scallion, finely chopped
1 egg
1/4 cup buttermilk

Garnish:
Cilantro
Parsley

You can use a grill or sauté pan to cook the seafood. Heat the oil and place the shrimp and scallops in the pan. Cook on each side for 2 to 3 minutes until lightly browned. Do not overcook the seafood. In a mixing bowl, combine all 4 ingredients for the chipotle butter and set aside. When ready to use, heat in a sauté pan.

To begin making the cornmeal pancakes, heat the vegetable oil in a large flat skillet over low heat. Meanwhile, mix all dry ingredients, then add the remaining ingredients and incorporate well. Drop batter on hot skillet to form pancakes. Turn with a spatula when they are ready.

Layer this dish like a Napoleon. Place a pancake centered on a plate, top with two scallops and a shrimp, then top with another pancake and two more scallops and a shrimp. Pour some of the hot chipotle butter over the top and garnish with a sprig of cilantro or parsley.

For a variety, try a Manog hot sauce from tortola or a passion fruit sauce from St. Thomas.

Servings: 4

Presented by: Beal House Inn and Restaurant - Littleton, New Hampshire

helpful hints . . .

Before storing fresh, uncooked shrimp, rinse them under cold, running water and drain thoroughly. Tightly cover and refrigerate for up to two days. Cooked shrimp can be refrigerated for up to three days. Shrimp can be frozen for up to three months. Thaw in its freezer wrapping overnight in the refrigerator, or place package in cold water until defrosted.

Personal touches . . .

sides, veggies & casseroles

helpful hints . . .

There are two main categories of onions: green onions, also called scallions, and dry onions. Dry onions are mature onions covered with a dry, papery texture and juicy flesh. Dry onions come in a wide range of sizes, shapes and flavors. Bermuda onions are a dry onion of mild flavoring and yellow or white in color. They are generally available March through June.

Personal touches . . .

_____

_____

_____

_____

_____

_____

Bermuda Onion Pie

1 frozen pastry sheet (10 x 17), defrosted
3 tablespoons olive oil
3 large Bermuda onions, halved and thinly sliced
Salt and fresh ground pepper to taste
1 clove garlic, thinly sliced
8 ounces Norwegian goat cheese, crumbled
8 to 10 ripe roma tomatoes, sliced about 1/4-inch thick
1 tablespoon extra virgin olive oil

Garnish:
Fresh rosemary
Fresh basil

Preheat oven to 375 degrees. Lightly flour and roll out pastry sheet to about a 15-inch circle, and fit into an 11-inch scalloped sided tart pan with removable bottom that has been lightly coated with a non-stick cooking spray. Trim excess dough, leaving a 1/2 inch overhang, then fold overhang inward and press against the side of pan to reinforce edge. Lightly prick holes in the bottom and sides with a fork. Line tart shell with aluminum foil and fill with pie weights or rice. Bake in the middle of oven for 15 to 20 minutes, or until edge becomes a pale golden color. Carefully remove pie weights and foil; bake until crust is golden all over. Cool tart shell in pan on a rack. While tart shell is baking, heat the olive oil in a heavy sauté pan over medium heat. Sauté onions, covered, for 15 to 20 minutes, until very soft. Add salt and pepper. Add garlic and continue to sauté, uncovered until onions are a dark purple and brown color.

Preheat broiler. Spread onion mixture over bottom of tart shell and top with 6 ounces of crumbled goat cheese. Arrange tomatoes, slightly overlapping, in concentric circles over cheese. Sprinkle with remaining cheese, salt and pepper and drizzle with the extra virgin olive oil. Place aluminum foil over edge of crust to prevent over browning. Place tart pan on baking sheet and place under broiler for about 5 to 6 minutes or until cheese and tomatoes turn brown. Garnish with fresh rosemary and basil.

Servings: 6 to 8

Presented by: The Wyman Hotel and Inn - Silverton, Colorado

Personal touches . . .

_____

_____

_____

_____

_____

_____

_____

Did you know . . . American potatoes are divided into four basic categories: russet, long white, round white and round red. Yukon gold potatoes, also known as boiling potatoes, have skin and flesh ranging from buttery yellow to golden and moist textures that make them excellent for mashed potatoes.

Crispy Potato Fritters

2 medium Yukon gold potatoes
1/2 medium white onion
2 tablespoons cornstarch
Salt to taste
Pepper to taste
Canola oil for pan-frying

Wash and quarter potatoes. Cut the white onion into 3 sections. Put both ingredients into a processor bowl and grate for a few seconds until coarse grate is attained. Move from processing bowl to a medium-sized mixing bowl. Add cornstarch, salt and pepper. Mix until well blended. Heat the canola oil in a frying skillet and fry fritters one at a time by a tablespoon measure. Flip and fry the other side until golden brown, draining each fritter carefully. Keep warm in an oven set at 250 degrees. Use 2 fritters per serving as a side for breakfast.

Servings: 4

Presented by: The Historic Inns of Abingdon: The Victoria & Albert Inn, The Love House Bed & Breakfast - Abingdon, Virginia

Personal touches . . .

_____

_____

_____

_____

_____

_____

_____

Confetti Potatoes

10 potatoes, chopped with skins
  (use a variety of types and colors)
1 large onion, chopped
1 cup peppers, chopped (all colors)
3 tablespoons olive oil
1 to 2 tablespoons Old Bay® Seasoning
1 tablespoon paprika
Dash of salt
Dash of pepper
Parsley, chopped (optional garnish)

Mix all ingredients. Bake at 375 degrees for 40 minutes or until potatoes are tender when pricked with fork. Stir a few times during cooking time. Adjust seasonings to taste, and sprinkle with chopped parsley before serving.

Servings: 12

Presented by: Celebrations Inn, a Festive Bed & Breakfast - Pomfret Center, Connecticut

Did you know . . . the flavor of paprika ranges from weak to strong and spicy. Most commercial paprika comes from California, Hungary, South America and Spain. The Hungarian variety is generally considered to be the most superior version. Mild paprika is available in all supermarkets, but for stronger, more pungent varieties, ethnic markets are usually the only resource. As with all herbs and spices, paprika should be stored in a cool, dark place and remains usable for up to six months.

Personal touches . . .

Did you know . . .
demi-glace is a rich
brown sauce that
begins with a basic
espagnole sauce. It is
combined with beef
stock and Madeira or
sherry and then
slowly cooked until it
is reduced by half to
a thick glaze that
coats a spoon. This
intense flavor is used
as a base for many
other sauces.

Wood Grilled Portobello Napoleons

8 large Portobello mushrooms, no stems
1 large sprig fresh rosemary
1/2 cup demi-glace
1/2 cup red wine
3 tablespoons vegetable oil
4 slices prosciutto
4 slices provolone or mozzarella
1 cup spinach, sautéed
1 garlic clove, minced
2 cups mashed potatoes

Garnish:
Rosemary sprig

Marinate the mushrooms overnight or at least 30 minutes in a large pan with rosemary, demi-glace and red wine. The next day, remove the mushrooms from the pan, and pat dry. Preheat oven to 350 degrees. Grill the mushrooms on each side for 2 minutes. If you do not have access to a grill, you can sauté them in a pan with 2-1/2 tablespoons of heated vegetable oil. Meanwhile, pour marinade into large pan and let simmer 4 to 5 minutes until reduced.

Personal
touches . . .

Remove the mushrooms from the grill or pan and place in the large pan filled with sauce. Top each mushroom with a slice of prosciutto and cheese. Slide into the oven for 2 to 3 minutes, or until the cheese has started to melt. Meanwhile, sauté the spinach with the garlic and 1/2 a tablespoon of vegetable oil. Remove the mushrooms from the oven; place a mound of mashed potatoes on them, top with sautéed spinach and the second mushroom cap. Spoon some of the demi-glace sauce over the mushroom and garnish with a piece of the rosemary sprig.

Servings: 4

Presented by: Beal House Inn and Restaurant -
Littleton, New Hampshire

Personal
touches . . .

_____

_____

_____

_____

_____

_____

_____

*Did you know . . .
fried green tomatoes
are a signature
Alabama side dish
and in general
considered a
Southern delicacy.*

Hughes Hacienda Fried Green Tomatoes

1/2 cup yellow cornmeal
1/2 cup brown sugar
1 teaspoon salt
1/2 teaspoon fresh ground pepper
1 large green tomato
1 egg, beaten
1 tablespoon butter

Mix the cornmeal, brown sugar, salt and pepper together on a plate. Cut the tomato in 1/2-inch slices; dip the slices in the beaten egg and lay the tomato slice in the cornmeal mixture to coat it on both sides. Melt the butter in an iron skillet and fry the tomatoes over medium heat just enough to brown each side. Serve hot.

Servings: 2

*Presented by: Hughes Hacienda Bed & Breakfast -
Colorado Springs, Colorado*

*Personal
touches . . .*

_____

_____

_____

_____

_____

_____

M*A*S*H™ Potato Cakes

5 to 6 cups grated potatoes
2 cups zucchini, grated or finely chopped
1 cup onion, grated or finely chopped
1 cup assorted bell peppers, chopped
1 cup seasoned Italian breadcrumbs
   (for wheat-free variety, prepare rice bread crumbs
   and add Italian seasonings to taste)
1/2 to 1 cup Parmesan cheese to taste, grated
1 to 2 tablespoons sun-dried tomatoes, finely chopped
2 tablespoons fresh parsley, chopped
1 tablespoon fresh French tarragon, chopped
2 large eggs
Salt and pepper to taste

Parboil potatoes with skin on until medium done, and allow to cool. In a large bowl, combine the potatoes and remaining ingredients, and mound into large meatball-like shapes. Place on lightly greased griddle heated to 350 to 400 degrees. Press into patty shapes. Cook approximately 4 minutes per side. Makes 20 to 25 3-inch cakes. Can be frozen and stored for up to 3 months.

Servings: 12

Presented by: A Creekside Garden Inn - Salem, Oregon

*Personal
touches . . .*

_____

_____

_____

_____

_____

_____

_____

helpful hints . . .

When cooking with zucchini, select smaller zucchini, which are young and tender with thinner skins. The skins should have vibrant color and be free of blemishes. Zucchini can be steamed, grilled, sautéed, deep-fried and baked.

*From the
Innkeeper...*
*"This is a recipe
that we serve for
Thanksgiving or
Christmas. It works
equally well with
turkey or prime rib.
Those that are
tentative about taking
a helping are always
sorry that they didn't
take more and just
leave the turkey to the
rest of the crowd."*
*– Innkeeper Karl
Schmitt*

Mushroom Casserole

1 pound mushrooms, sliced
1/4 cup beef broth (canned) or 1 cube beef bullion
    dissolved in 1/4 cup water
2 tablespoons flour
1/2 cup cream
1/2 teaspoon salt or to taste
1/2 cup breadcrumbs
1/2 to 3/4 cup Parmesan cheese
4 to 6 teaspoons butter

Place mushrooms in casserole pan and set aside. In a sauce pan, combine beef broth/bullion and flour, and cook over medium high heat. Add cream and salt. In a separate bowl, mix together breadcrumbs and Parmesan cheese. Pour sauce over mushrooms, top with crumbs and dot with butter. Bake at 350 degrees for 45 minutes.

Servings: 6 to 8

*Presented by: Casa de San Pedro Bed & Breakfast -
Hereford, Arizona*

*Personal
touches . . .*

Asparagus Casserole

1 bag wide egg noodles
2 cans asparagus, drained (or equivalent amount of fresh)
4 cans cream of mushroom soup
2 pounds Velveeta® cheese, cubed

Cook egg noodles per product directions. If using fresh asparagus, cook until tender. Combine all ingredients and pour into casserole dish evenly. Bake at 350 degrees for 30 minutes or until bubbly and lightly browned on edges.

Servings: 6 to 8

Presented by: Alaska Gold Rush Bed & Breakfast Inn - Palmer, Alaska

Personal touches . . .

_____

_____

_____

_____

_____

_____

*Did you know . . .
the potato was
originally thought to
be poisonous because
it was considered a
member of the
nightshade family.
In the 16th century,
Sir Walter Raleigh
was influential in
exposing the
superstition as
fictitious by planting
them on his property
in Ireland.*

Oven Home Fries

6 to 8 red potatoes, sliced
1 onion, sliced
Salt to taste
Pepper to taste
1 tablespoon mustard
1/4 cup olive oil

Toss all ingredients in a bowl. Place on a large baking sheet. Bake at 450 degrees for about 45 minutes.

Potatoes can also be cooked on a pre-greased griddle. Optional additional ingredients include Italian seasoning or seasoning salt.

Servings: 6 to 8

Presented by: John F. Craig House - Cape May, New Jersey

*Personal
touches . . .*

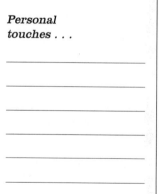

_____

_____

_____

_____

_____

_____

Arrington's
Bed & Breakfast Journal
Trade Information For the B&B and Country Inn Innkeeper, Innsitter and Aspiring Owner

June 2004 • $5.00

Attracting Business Travelers

www.bnbjournal.com

Arrington's Bed & Breakfast Journal® is a monthly industry trade publication for the bed & breakfast and country inn innkeeper, innsitter and aspiring owner. It is the leading resource magazine for the B&B/country inn industry. Each month, it is our goal to provide industry resource information, feature articles and columns that are substantive, interesting and readily applicable to daily B&B/country inn operations. We also feature a real estate department to help you find that perfect establishment; recipes; an eclectic array of advice from industry experts; and other insightful information.

If you are an innkeeper looking for new ideas and avenues on how to increase your business, or if you are an aspiring owner needing some startup advice or an innsitter looking for your next assignment, *Arrington's Bed & Breakfast Journal®* is the resource magazine you are looking for!

YES! Send me Arrington's Bed & Breakfast Journal®!

☐ **1** year (12 issues) only $29.00

Texas Residents 1 year - $31.39
Canadian Residents 1 year - $30.00

Name _____ _ _ _ _

Address _____ Apt. _____ _ _ _ _

City _____ State _____ Zip _ _ _ _

E-mail _____ _ _ _ _

Payment Enclosed ☐   Bill Me Later ☐

Remit to:
Arrington Publishing, 214 W. Texas, Suite 400, Midland, Texas 79701

fruits

Jim's Sautéed Apples

3 tablespoons butter
1 cup brown sugar, loosely packed
1 cup hard apple cider (B.F. Clyde's® or local producer)
2 medium or large apples
   (Cortland, Macintosh, etc.), sliced
Cinnamon
Vanilla yogurt or cream (optional)

Peel and core the apples and slice thinly (1/4 inch). In a sauté pan or large non-stick fry pan, melt the first 3 ingredients, stirring until sugar is dissolved. Bring sauce to a full boil and add apple. Reduce heat to simmer and cook apples, stirring infrequently so as not to break up slices, until apples are tender and sauce is reduced by about 75 percent. Sprinkle with cinnamon before serving. May be served either hot or cold with a dollop of vanilla yogurt or a splash of cream.

Servings: 2

Presented by: Another Second Penny Inn -
Stonington, Connecticut

Did you know . . .
B.F. Clyde® is the oldest continuous producer of hard cider in the United States. The company has been family owned and operated since 1881, and the mill is the last steam powered cedar mill in the United States. A recent recipient of a National Historic Mechanical Engineering Landmark Award, B.F. Clyde® produces fresh cider daily during the fall and is also a bonded winery, producing hard ciders and apple wines.

Personal touches . . .

_____

_____

_____

_____

_____

_____

Brandied Bananas

4 small to medium bananas, slightly under-ripe
  produce the best presentation
2 tablespoons butter
1-1/2 ounces brandy
2 tablespoons cinnamon sugar
  (1/4 cup sugar combined with 1 teaspoon cinnamon)
1/2 teaspoon ground nutmeg
3 ounces almonds, slivered

Peel bananas and slice in half crosswise and then length-wise to make 4 pieces each; there should be 16 slices total. Melt butter and coat bottom of two 10-inch skillets. Place pans on burners set to medium high. Place 8 pieces of banana, flat side down, into each skillet. Allow slices to brown until just golden, approximately 1-1/2 minutes. Turn slices so that flat side faces up, and reduce heat to low. Pour brandy over slices, and immediately sprinkle cinnamon sugar over each slice. Add nutmeg in pinches to each slice until evenly distributed. Remove slices to serving plates and top with slivered almonds. Serve immediately.

Servings: 4

Presented by: The Painted Lady Bed and Breakfast - Elmira, New York

Personal touches . . .

_____

_____

_____

_____

_____

helpful hints . . .

When selecting bananas, choose plump, evenly colored yellow bananas flecked with tiny brown specks, a sign of ripeness. Avoid bananas with blemishes, which are usually bruised. Bananas with greenish tips and ridges will need further ripening at home. Bananas are low in fat and proteins, high in carbohydrates and rich in vitamin C and potassium.

Poached Pears in Chambord

Did you know. . .
pears are a great
source of natural
dietary fiber. One
pear provides 16
percent of the
recommended daily
allowance of fiber.

4 pears, peeled, cut in half and cored
4 tablespoons brown sugar
2 tablespoons cinnamon
2 tablespoons Chambord (raspberry liquor)
4 tablespoons wine
2 tablespoons blueberries
2 tablespoons raspberries
Cheddar, bleu or feta cheese to top

Place the pears cored side up in glass baking dish. Sprinkle sugar and cinnamon over pears. Pour Chambord and wine over them, and divide berries among pears. Cover tightly with plastic wrap and microwave on high 10 minutes. Serve warm with sauce and a sprinkling of cheese. You can use fresh, frozen or dried berries for this recipe.

Servings: 4

Presented by: Desert Willow Bed & Breakfast -
Jemez Springs, New Mexico

Personal
touches . . .

_____

_____

_____

_____

_____

_____

_____

Spiced Apples

1 cup cranberry juice
6 to 8 Granny Smith apples, sliced
1 teaspoon cinnamon
1/2 cup sugar
1 tablespoon cornstarch
Red hot candies (optional)

Place cranberry juice in large frying pan. Place apples in frying pan. In a separate bowl, combine cinnamon, sugar and cornstarch. Sprinkle over apples. Add red hot candies; they will make the apples a pretty red color. Cover with a lid and cook until the apples are tender. These are fabulous with baked French toast.

Servings: 4 to 6

Presented by: The John F. Craig House Bed & Breakfast - Cape May, New Jersey

Personal touches . . .

_____

_____

_____

_____

_____

_____

helpful hints . . .

Granny Smith apples were named after Maria (or Mary) Ann Smith, an Australian gardener who discovered the apples. It is said that she found the seedling growing where she had discarded some apples and began using the fruit for cooking. It is thought that the seedling originally came from the seed of a French Crabapple. Granny Smith apples are a great all-purpose apple with a firm, crisp flesh and a pleasantly tart flavor.

Peaches Lewis

4 quarts water
1 large bowl of ice water
4 large ripe peaches, skinned
1/4 cup unsalted butter, chopped
1/3 cup dark brown sugar
2 tablespoons brandy
Homemade vanilla ice cream (or quality store bought)

Bring 4 quarts water to boil, and have a large bowl of ice water handy. Boil each peach for 6 to 10 seconds; immediately remove peach from boiling water and submerge in ice water to stop cooking. Remove skin, slice into 10 sections and set aside. In a large, heavy skillet over medium heat, melt butter and blend in brown sugar. Cook for 1 minute while stirring. Add peaches and cook on one side for about 1 minute. Turn peaches over, add brandy and ignite. Cook peaches for 2 minutes. Place 2 scoops ice cream in the center of a large plate, arrange 10 peach sections around ice cream and pour liquid on top of ice cream.

Servings: 4

Presented by: The Wyman Hotel & Inn - Silverton, Colorado

Did you know . . . peaches are members of the rose family. The two basic categories of peaches are freestone and clingstone. Freestone peaches have a pit from which the flesh is easily removed, and clingstone peaches have a pit to which the flesh adheres. Peaches are the state fruit of South Carolina and Georgia. Johnston, South Carolina, is regarded as the "Peach Capital of the World."

Personal touches . . .

_____
_____
_____
_____
_____
_____
_____

Chalet Suzanne's Broiled Grapefruit

1 grapefruit, at room temperature
3 tablespoons butter
1 teaspoon sugar
4 tablespoons cinnamon-sugar
    (1/4 cup sugar combined with 1 teaspoon cinnamon)

Preheat broiler. Slice grapefruit in half and cut membrane around the center of fruit. Cut around each section, close to the membrane, so that the fruit is completely loosened from its shell. Fill the center of each half with 1-1/2 table-spoons of butter. Sprinkle 1/2 a teaspoon of sugar over each grapefruit half, then sprinkle each with 2 tablespoons of cinnamon sugar. Place grapefruit on a shallow baking pan. Broil just long enough to brown tops and heat until bubbling. Remove from oven and serve hot.

Servings: 2

Presented by: Chalet Suzanne Country Inn & Restaurant - Lake Whales, Florida

Personal touches . . .

_____

_____

_____

_____

_____

_____

Breeden Inn's Applesauce

4 medium apples (use a variety) pared,
   quartered and cored
1 cup water
1/2 cup brown sugar, packed
1/4 teaspoon cinnamon
1/8 teaspoon nutmeg

Boil apples over medium heat in water. Reduce heat. Simmer, stirring occasionally for 5 to 10 minutes or until tender. Stir in brown sugar, cinnamon and nutmeg. Heat to a boil, and stir while boiling for 2 minutes. Serve with biscuits or other homemade breads.

Servings: 4 cups

Presented by: The Breeden Inn Bed & Breakfast - Bennettsville, South Carolina

Did you know... the world production of apples is more than 40 million tons? European countries consume about 46 pounds of apples annually, while Americans eat about 19.6 pounds of fresh apples annually. China and the United States are the world's largest apple producers. Apples are the second most valuable fruit crop in the United States. The first recorded planting of apples in the United States was in 1629 by the Massachusetts Bay Colony.

Personal touches . . .

_____
_____
_____
_____
_____
_____

Did you know...
blueberries are great
additions to a healthy
diet, with significant
quantities of antiviral
and antibacterial
compounds. They are
also said to aid in
protection from heart
disease. Over 200
million pounds of
blueberries are
grown commercially
each year. Maine
produces roughly 25
percent of all the
blueberries, both wild
and cultivated
combined, in North
America. They are
the largest producers
of wild blueberries in
the world with over
60,000 acres of
blueberry crops
throughout the state.

Personal
touches . . .

Blueberry Buckle

1/4 cup butter
3/4 cup sugar
2 eggs
1 teaspoon vanilla extract
2 cups flour
2 teaspoons baking powder
1/2 teaspoon salt
1/2 cup buttermilk (regular milk can also be used)
2-1/2 cups blueberries
1/2 cup brown sugar
1 teaspoon cinnamon
1/4 cup nuts

Cream butter and sugar, beat in eggs and vanilla. Combine flour, baking powder and salt. Add flour mixture and buttermilk alternately to sugar mixture. Stir in berries. Spread batter in 9-inch pan. In a separate bowl, combine brown sugar, cinnamon and nuts. Sprinkle mixture on top of batter. Bake at 375 degrees for 25 to 30 minutes.

Servings: 4 to 6

Presented by: The John F. Craig House Bed & Breakfast - Cape May, New Jersey

Triple Ginger Baked Pears

10 assorted pears, cored and coarsely chopped
6 tablespoons butter
1/2 cup brown sugar
2 teaspoons ground ginger
1/2 box of gingersnap cookies, crumbled
1/4 cup crystallized ginger, chopped

Toss first 4 ingredients in a shallow baking dish. Bake at 350 degrees for 20 minutes or until tender when pricked with fork. Turn pears 2 to 3 times during cooking time to ensure pears cook evenly. Place 1/4 cup of gingersnap cookies in bottom of individual dishes. Spoon baked pears over cookies. Sprinkle the top of the pears with crystallized ginger.

Servings: 8 to 10

Presented by: Celebrations Inn, a Festive Bed & Breakfast - Pomfret Center, Connecticut

Did you know...
the powdered, dried form of ginger is more intense and spicy in flavor than fresh varieties. It is often used in baked goods such as ginger cookies, gingersnaps and gingerbread. Ginger is available in various forms beyond fresh and dried. Try experimenting with crystallized, candied, preserved and the pickled version. Ginger is said to combat motion sickness more effectively than-over-the-counter medication.

Personal touches . . .

Baked Banana Crumble

3/4 cup orange juice
1 teaspoon vanilla extract
4 ripe bananas, peeled, cut in half and cut lengthwise
1/2 cup flour
1/2 cup quick cooking oatmeal
3/4 cup brown sugar
1/2 teaspoon nutmeg
6 tablespoons butter, cubed

Combine orange juice and vanilla in baking dish. Add bananas, spooning juice over them. In a bowl, combine dry ingredients. Using a fork or pastry blender, add the butter until the mixture resembles small peas. Spoon crumble over fruit. Bake at 325 degrees until the bananas soften, approximately 7 to 10 minutes. Do not over bake; the bananas will turn an unappetizing color. This recipe can also be prepared in individual greased ramekins and served with a dollop of whipped cream.

Servings: 5

Presented by: Wander Inn - Newport, Rhode Island

Personal touches . . .

_____

_____

_____

_____

_____

_____

cakes & pies

Coconut Lime Buttermilk Pie

2 cups sugar
1 cup sweetened shredded coconut
3/4 cup buttermilk
2/3 cup coconut milk
1/2 tablespoon flour
3 eggs
3 egg yolks
1 teaspoon vanilla
Juice of 1 lime
1 pie shell, unbaked

Preheat oven to 350 degrees. Whisk all ingredients together in large bowl until well mixed. Place unbaked pie shell in an 8-1/2-inch deep pie dish, and pour batter into shell. Place on baking sheet and bake for 40 to 50 minutes or until filling is just set, but still jiggly. Remove from oven and cool to room temperature. Chill if not serving right away.

Servings: 6 to 8

Presented by: Casa de San Pedro Bed & Breakfast Inn - Hereford, Arizona

Personal touches . . .

Hard Apple Cider Cake

This recipe dates back to the 1830s and is quite similar to a pound cake.

6 cups flour
1 teaspoon baking soda
1/2 teaspoon salt
1 teaspoon nutmeg, grated
1 cup butter, softened
3 cups sugar
4 eggs
1 cup cider (B.F. Clyde's® Hard Apple Cider non-sparkling version works best, but any good cider will work; something dry rather than sweet is best.)

Preheat oven to 350 degrees and grease 2 regular-sized loaf pans or 4 small loaf pans. In a bowl, mix together flour, soda, salt and nutmeg; set aside. Using an electric mixer, cream butter well. Add sugar gradually, creaming until fluffy, then add eggs one at a time and beat thoroughly. On low or "stir" speed, add the flour mixture alternately with the cider, beating until smooth after each addition. Distribute batter evenly in loaf pans. Bake for about 1 hour; gas ovens may take up to 10 minutes longer. Inserted toothpick should come out clean. Keep moist with a chunk of apple in the container. Freezes well.

Servings: 2 regular-sized loaves or 4 small loaves

Presented by: Another Second Penny Inn - Stonington, Connecticut

Personal touches . . .

_____

_____

_____

_____

_____

_____

Coconut Lover's Cake

1 package white cake mix
3 eggs, separated
2 tablespoons oil
1/4 teaspoon almond extract
1-1/2 cups milk
2 cups Angel Flake® coconut
1 can (15 ounces) cream of coconut
1 large container (9 ounces) Cool Whip®

Preheat oven to 350 degrees. Lightly grease a 9 x 13 baking dish. In a separate bowl, combine cake mix, egg whites, oil, flavoring and milk. Add one cup of the coconut to the batter and reserve the remainder. Pour batter into baking dish and bake 20 to 25 minutes or until done. Make holes in warm cake about 1 inch apart with the handle of a wooden spoon. Pour the can of the cream of coconut over cake and cool. Combine second cup of coconut and Cool Whip®. Spread over the top of cake as you would icing. Cake is best stored in refrigerator.

Servings: 1 cake

Presented by: Alaska Gold Rush Bed & Breakfast Inn - Palmer, Alaska

Did you know... there are over 20 billion coconuts produced each year. Until soybean oil took over in the 1960s, coconut oil was the worlds leading vegetable oil. Coconuts are thought to have originated in the region around New Guinea in the Pacific Ocean, but many botanists believe they could have originated in the American tropics. Each theory is considered merely speculation, as there is no proof of either origin.

Personal touches . . .

_____
_____
_____
_____
_____
_____
_____

Devon Cream Cheese Pie with Berries

Wonderful with English tea!

2 (8-ounce) packages cream cheese, room temperature
1/2 cup granulated sugar
1-1/2 teaspoons vanilla
2 packages of crescent-style dinner rolls
1 cup fresh or frozen blueberries
   (substitute other fruit if desired)
1/4 cup butter, melted
Cinnamon sugar (1/4 cup sugar
   combined with 1 teaspoon cinnamon)

Garnish and Accompaniments:
1 jar Devon or clotted cream (optional)
Fresh mint sprigs

Preheat oven to 350 degrees and butter a 9 x 15 baking dish. Whip the cream cheese, sugar and vanilla together; set aside. Cover the bottom of the baking dish with one layer of dinner roll dough (1 can), pinching the dough to keep it together as one layer. Spread the sweetened cream cheese over the dough. Top with berries.

Personal touches . . .

_____

_____

_____

_____

_____

_____

Cover the cream cheese filling with berries and top with another layer of crescent dough (1 can). Pour the melted butter on top and sprinkle generously with cinnamon sugar. Bake for 20 to 30 minutes or until golden brown. Let cool before serving. Serve with a dollop of Devon or clotted cream, topped with a spring of fresh mint.

Servings: 6 to 8

Presented by: Inn Britannia - Searsport, Maine

Devonshire cream or clotted cream is a traditional accompaniment to English cream tea and usually served with jam and scones. To make Devonshire or clotted cream, warm 2 cups cream in the top of a double boiler over simmering water until cream is reduced by about half. Its consistency should be similar to butter with a golden crust on the surface. Transfer cream into a bowl, cover and allow to cool for 2 hours and refrigerate for at least 12 hours. Stir before using and keep any unused portions tightly covered in refrigerator.

Personal touches . . .

_____

_____

_____

_____

_____

_____

_____

*Did you know...
the term pound
cake originated from
an original recipe,
which called for one
pound of each
ingredient: butter,
sugar, eggs and
flour.*

Cream Cheese Poundcake

1-1/2 cups butter, softened
1 (8-ounce) package cream cheese
3 cups sugar
6 large eggs
1-1/2 teaspoons vanilla
3 cups all-purpose flour
1/8 teaspoon salt

Preheat oven to 300 degrees, and grease and flour a 10-inch tube pan or 3 – 8 x 4 loaf pans. In a bowl, beat butter and cream cheese at medium speed until creamy. Gradually add sugar, beating 5 to 7 minutes. Add eggs, one at a time, beating just until yellow disappears. Add vanilla and mix well. In a separate bowl, combine flour and salt. Gradually add to butter mixture, beating at a low speed until just blended. Pour batter into tube or loaf pans. Place in oven and bake for 1 hour and 10 minutes. Fill a 2-cup Pyrex measuring cup with water and place in oven with cake during baking duration.

Servings: 1 tube cake or 3 loaves

Presented by: The John F. Craig House Bed & Breakfast - Cape May, New Jersey

*Personal
touches . . .*

_____

_____

_____

_____

_____

_____

The following is a version of an original recipe from Hanna Glasse's "Art of Cookery Made Plain and Easy," published in 1747.

*"To Make a Pound Cake
Take a pound of butter, beat it in an earthen pan with your hand one way, till it is like a fine thick cream: then have ready twelve eggs, but half the whites; beat them well, and beat them up with the butter, a pound of flour beat in it, a pound of sugar, and a few carraways. Beat it all well together for an hour with your hand, or a great wooden spoon, butter a pan and put it in, and then bake it an hour in a quick oven. For a change you may put in a pound of currants, clean washed and picked."*

cookies & pastries

Congo Squares

2/3 cup butter or margarine
2-1/2 cups brown sugar, packed (1 pound)
2-2/3 cups sifted flour
2-1/2 teaspoons baking powder
1/2 teaspoon salt
3 eggs
1 cup nuts, chopped
1 cup Nestlé® semi-sweet chocolate morsels

Preheat oven to 350 degrees and grease a 10 x 15 baking pan. Heat a sauce pan over medium high heat and melt butter or margarine. Stir in brown sugar. Remove from heat and cool 10 minutes. In a separate bowl, sift together flour, baking powder and salt. Beat in each of the 3 eggs, one at a time. Stir in flour mixture. Add nuts and chocolate morsels, and spread into greased baking dish. Bake 25 to 30 minutes. Cool and cut into squares.

Servings: 3 dozen 2-inch squares

Presented by: Mill Creek Homestead Bed & Breakfast - Bird-in-Hand, Pennsylvania

Personal touches . . .

_____
_____
_____
_____
_____
_____
_____

*Did you know...
apples are a good
source of vitamins A
and C. Remember,
"an apple a day keeps
the doctor away!"*

Catherine's Tarte Tatin

8 large apples (combine Red Delicious and
    Granny Smith or Golden Delicious and Cortland)
3 peaches
8-ounce puff pastry sheet
1/2 cup sugar
1 teaspoon vanilla

Peel and core the apples; cut each into 4 sections. Cut 1 peach into 4 sections. Cut the other 2 into 8 slices each and set aside. Trim the puff pastry sheet into a circle, and roll it out on a lightly floured surface until it has a diameter of at least 12 inches. Let it stand at room temperature while you place the sugar and vanilla in a large 10-inch oven-proof sauté pan. Heat on a medium setting until ingredients are combined and they turn a caramel color, approximately 4 to 5 minutes. Immediately remove pan from heat; be careful not to overcook or the sugar will burn, as it continues to cook even after you remove it from the heat.

*Personal
touches . . .*

_____

_____

_____

_____

_____

_____

Be careful, as the pan and caramel are extremely hot. Place the 4 peach sections in the center of the pan, and then place apple sections and peach slices around it in a circle, alternating the fruit. Finish off with a second layer of apples. Pick up the puff pastry sheet and drape over the top of the pan, crimping the edges into the pan's rim. Bake for 30 to 40 minutes or until the top of the pastry is golden brown and crisp. After the tarte comes out of the oven, invert it onto a large plate. Be careful, as there will be some juices in the bottom of the pan. You can drain these off carefully before turning the tarte over. Serve.

Although this tarte tastes wonderful on its own, you can serve it with a scoop of berry sorbet or French vanilla or cinnamon ice cream. Besides apple and peach, try combining kiwi, mango, papaya, etc.

Servings: 8

Presented by: Beal House Inn and Restaurant - Littleton, New Hampshire

Personal touches . . .

_____

_____

_____

_____

_____

_____

_____

Did you know...
Late Harvest Riesling
wine is pale-straw in
color with an essence
of superb balance
between sweetness
and acidity. It has a
floral nose that hints
of citrus blossoms,
peaches and melons.
It is an exquisite
accompaniment to
cheese and Asian
dishes.

"Wine Coins" Yakima Valley Wine Country Cookies

1/2 cup unsalted butter
2 tablespoons Late Harvest Riesling wine
1/2 cup sugar
3 egg yolks
2 cups all-purpose flour
Confectioners' sugar, for dusting

In a bowl, beat butter and wine together at a high speed until creamy. Add sugar and 1 egg yolk at a time, beating well after each addition. Mix in flour and beat for 1 minute. Shape dough into a flat ball. Cover with plastic wrap and refrigerate for 30 minutes.

Preheat oven to 350 degrees. On a lightly floured surface, roll out refrigerated dough to 1/4-inch thickness. Flour a 2-3/4-inch smooth, round cookie cutter. Place cut dough 1 inch apart on ungreased baking sheets. Bake 10 to 12 minutes or until edges are golden. Remove cookies from baking sheets to cool on wire racks. Sprinkle cookies with confectioners' sugar, and they are ready to enjoy.

Servings: 2 dozen

Presented by: A Touch of Europe® Bed & Breakfast and Fine Dining - Yakima, Washington

Personal touches . . .

Cream Puffs & Chocolate Sauce

Cream Puffs:
1/2 cup butter
1 cup water
1 cup sifted all-purpose flour
1/4 teaspoon salt
4 eggs
2 cups whipping cream, whipped and sweetened

Chocolate Sauce:
1 cup sugar
2 tablespoons cocoa
2 tablespoons butter
1 small can evaporated milk
1 teaspoon vanilla

Cream Puffs
In a saucepan, combine butter and water, and bring to vigorous boil. Sift together flour and salt. Reduce heat to low, and add flour and salt. Stir vigorously until mixture lifts from the sides of pan and forms a stiff ball. Remove from heat. Add eggs one at a time, beating hard after each addition. Drop by tablespoons or cookie press to form puffs about 2 to 2-1/2 inches in diameter on greased cookie sheets. Bake at 450 degrees for 15 minutes, and then 325 degrees for 20 minutes. Remove to cooling racks.

Chocolate Sauce
Put sugar, cocoa and butter in sauce pan. Heat on low for 2 minutes. Add evaporated milk, and slowly bring to a boil. Boil 1 minute. Remove from heat and add vanilla. When puffs have cooled, cut a hole in the side of each and fill with whipped cream or ice cream and drizzle with chocolate sauce.

Servings: 4 to 6

Presented by: The John F. Craig House Bed & Breakfast - Cape May, New Jersey

Personal touches . . .

_____

_____

_____

_____

_____

_____

Napoleons with Eggnog Custard and Caramelized Apples

Eggnog Custard:
1 cup whole milk
1/2 cup eggnog (available at liquor stores)
2 egg yolks
3 tablespoons superfine sugar
   (available in baking section at supermarket)
4 tablespoons cornstarch
Confectioners' sugar

Caramelized Apples:
5 tablespoons unsalted butter
5 tablespoons superfine sugar
5 large apples (Golden Delicious or Pink Lady) peeled,
   cored and cut into 1/4-inch thick slices
2 tablespoons Calvados® or Applejack® (available in
   liquor stores)

Puff Pastry:
1 sheet puff pastry, thawed at room temperature
   (about 15 minutes)
8 teaspoons sugar
Confectioners' sugar

Personal touches . . .

_____

_____

_____

_____

_____

_____

Eggnog Custard
Bring milk and eggnog to a boil in a non-stick medium saucepan. In a medium bowl, beat egg yolks and sugar until creamy. Stir in the cornstarch, continuing to stir while pouring the hot milk mixture into the egg yolk mixture. Pour bowl contents into the same saucepan and carefully simmer on very low heat for 1 to 2 minutes, stirring constantly to avoid boiling or burning. Pour cream mixture into a heat-proof glass bowl and lightly dust with confectioners' sugar, or press a round piece of plastic wrap directly on surface of custard to prevent a film or crust from forming. Refrigerate until chilled, about 3 to 4 hours. Can also be made 1 day ahead.

Caramelized Apples

Heat butter and sugar in a large non-stick skillet. Cook over medium heat until mixture forms a light caramel. Add apple slices, and turn heat to medium high. Brown apple slices evenly on all sides. Once apples are soft, add Calvados or Applejack, briefly flambé and remove from heat.

Note: If you prefer to forego the flambéing step, cook apples a little longer to incorporate alcohol into the apple mixture. If you prefer to flambé, exercise extreme caution when doing so.

Puff Pastry

Line a large baking sheet with parchment paper. Roll out pastry sheet on a lightly floured surface to a 12-inch square. Cut pastry into 4 – 5-inch squares, cut each square diagonally into triangles, then transfer to the prepared baking sheet. Prick each triangle with a fork, sprinkle them with 1 teaspoon of sugar and refrigerate for 10 minutes.

Preheat oven to 375 degrees. Bake 15 to 20 minutes or until puffed and golden brown. Transfer pastry from the baking sheet to a wire rack to cool. On a cutting board, cut each triangle lengthwise in half. Place bottom halves on dessert plates, top each with 2 to 3 tablespoons of eggnog custard. Top custard with apple slices, then with the other half of pastry. Dust each serving with confectioners' sugar. Arrange any remaining slices around the edges of each Napoleon along with a drizzling of caramel sauce and enjoy.

Servings: 8

Presented by: A Touch of Europe® Bed & Breakfast and Fine Dining - Yakima, Washington

Did you know... there are many theories and speculations concerning the origins of napoleons. Danish folklore imparts that a royal Danish pastry chef invented the napoleon during the 1800s for the occasion of a state visit between the King of Denmark and Emperor Napoleon. French origin versions of the napoleon state that Emperor Napoleon ate so many of the pastries on the eve of Waterloo that he ended up losing the battle.

Personal touches . . .

_____

_____

_____

_____

_____

_____

_____

mousse & parfaits

Swedish Cream

2 teaspoons gelatin
1 tablespoon cold water
1-1/2 cups heavy cream
1/2 cup sugar
1/4 cup plain yogurt
3/4 cup sour cream
1/2 teaspoon vanilla
2 tablespoons Grand Marnier®
Fresh berries
Whipped cream

Soften gelatin in water in saucepan. When soft, add heavy cream and sugar. Put pan on medium heat, and stir until gelatin dissolves. Do not boil. Let cook for 20 minutes, stirring occasionally. Fold in yogurt, sour cream, vanilla and Grand Marnier®. Pour into parfait glasses. Top with berries and a rosette of whipped cream.

Servings: 2 to 4

Presented by: A La Provence Bed & Breakfast - Freeland, Washington

Personal touches . . .

_____

_____

_____

_____

_____

_____

White Chocolate Raspberry Dream Terrine

1-1/4 cups raspberry purée
1 tablespoon Chambord®
8 ounces quality white chocolate, chopped
3/4 cup sugar
1-1/3 cups water
1 tablespoon light corn syrup
4 large egg whites
2 cups whip cream, chilled
1 teaspoon vanilla extract

Line a 9 x 5 x 3 loaf pan with aluminum foil, extending the foil over the sides. Transfer the raspberry purée to a small bowl and add the Chambord®. Using a double broiler, melt the white chocolate and remove from heat. Combine sugar, water and corn syrup in a sauce pan and stir until all of the sugar has dissolved. Boil for 3 to 4 minutes or until a candy thermometer reaches 250 degrees. In a separate bowl, beat the egg whites until soft peaks form, and gradually add the sugar syrup to the whites, beating until firm peaks form. Fold the melted white chocolate into the meringue.

Beat the whipping cream with vanilla until firm peaks form, and fold into the above meringue. Transfer half of the mixture into a large bowl and add the raspberry purée. Spread half of this raspberry mixture into the bottom of the loaf pan and freeze for 20 minutes. Add all of the white chocolate mousse to the loaf pan and freeze for another 20 minutes. Spread the last layer of raspberry mousse, cover with plastic and freeze overnight. When ready to serve, uncover the terrine and loosen the sides by cutting between the foil and the pan. Invert onto a large platter, and serve with dark chocolate sauce on the side or slice the terrine for individual servings.

Servings: 8

Presented by: Beal House Inn and Restaurant - Littleton, New Hampshire

Did you know...
white chocolate is not really chocolate at all. In general, white chocolate is a combination of sugar, cocoa butter, milk solids, lecithin and vanilla. The reason it is not classified as chocolate is because there is no amount of chocolate liquor in it, which means there is also very little chocolate flavor. When cooking with white chocolate, remember it must be melted very slowly over low heat to keep it from scorching and clumping.

Personal touches . . .

_____

_____

_____

_____

_____

Strawberries Romanoff

1 quart fresh strawberries, halved
2 tablespoons sugar
1 pint strawberry ice cream
1/2 cup sour cream or yogurt
2 tablespoons orange liqueur, GranGala® works well

Sprinkle berries with sugar. Cover and chill. Meanwhile, stir ice cream until softened. Fold in sour cream or yogurt and liqueur. Cover and freeze 1 hour or overnight. To serve, top each serving of berries with a generous dollop of ice cream mixture in a pretty parfait or other serving dish.

Servings: 4

Presented by: Wander Inn - Newport, Rhode Island

Personal touches . . .

_____

_____

_____

_____

_____

_____

helpful hints . . .

Strawberries should only be purchased a few days prior to use, as they are extremely perishable. When choosing berries, look for firm, plump strawberries that are free of mold with a deep, shiny red color and attached green caps. The large strawberries are usually not as flavorful as medium-sized berries. Strawberries should always be stored in the refrigerator, as exposure to sunlight or room temperature for too long will cause them to spoil.

Measurements and Conversion Table

Teaspoons	Tablespoons	Cups	Fluid Ounces	Milliliters	Other
1/4 teaspoon				1 ml	
1/2 teaspoon				2 ml	
3/4 teaspoon	1/4 tablespoon			4 ml	
1 teaspoon	1/3 tablespoon			5 ml	
3 teaspoons	1 tablespoon	1/16 cup	1/2 oz	15 ml	
6 teaspoons	2 tablespoons	1/8 cup	1 oz	30 ml	
			1-1/2 oz	44 ml	1 jigger
12 teaspoons	4 tablespoons	1/4 cup	2 oz	60 ml	
16 teaspoons	5-1/3 tablespoons	1/3 cup	2-1/2 oz	75 ml	
18 teaspoons	6 tablespoons	3/8 cup	3 oz	90 ml	
24 teaspoons	8 tablespoons	1/2 cup	4 oz	125 ml	1/4 pint
32 teaspoons	10-2/3 tablespoons	2/3 cup	5 oz	150 ml	
36 teaspoons	12 tablespoons	3/4 cup	6 oz	175 ml	
48 teaspoons	16 tablespoons	1 cup	8 oz	237 ml	1/2 pint
		1-1/2 cups	12 oz	355 ml	
		2 cups	16 oz	473 ml	1 pint
		3 cups	24 oz	710 ml	1-1/2 pints
			25.6 oz	757 ml	1 fifth
		4 cups	32 oz	946 ml	1 quart / 1 liter
		8 cups	64 oz		2 quarts
		16 cups	128 oz		1 gallon

1 pinch or dash - What can be picked up between thumb and first two fingers; less than 1/8 teaspoon.

1/2 pinch - What can be picked up between thumb and one finger.

To substitute a glass pan for baking, reduce baking temperature by 25 degrees.

To substitute a pan that is deeper than the pan required in the recipe, increase the baking time by one-fourth.

To substitute a pan that is shallower than the pan required in the recipe, decrease the baking time by one-fourth.

Spice & Seasoning Guide

Allspice – A spice with delicate flavoring that resembles a blend of nutmeg, cinnamon and cloves. Use in puddings, fruit preserves, baking, meats and pickles.

Arrowroot – Powder made from the root of a South American plant used for thickening fruit sauces and glazes. Mild in flavor and excellent for flavoring food for infants and children.

Anise – A strong licorice flavored spice used to enhance coffeecake, sweet rolls, candies and pickles.

Basil – An aromatic spice with leafy flavoring. Popular for seasoning tomato dishes as well as vegetables, lamb and poultry. Use in salad dressings, marinades and dips, hot or cold, pasta and otherwise bland vegetables.

Bay leaves – A sweet, herbaceous spice with a touch of floral. Use in all bean and vegetable stews and sauces as well as meat and fish dishes. Enhances a rustic flavor in onion, potato, squash and rice dishes.

Caraway – A spice that encompasses the flavor combination of anise and dill. Often used in baked breads, cheese spreads, applesauce, salads, noodles and sauerkraut. Try adding it to canned asparagus or French fries for extra pizzazz.

Cardamom – A spice closely related to ginger. Available ground or as whole seeds or seed pods. Used in pork marinades, on cabbage, carrots or with fruits such as citrus fruit salads.

Cayenne pepper – A very strong spice that should be used minimally. Popular for seasoning Louisiana and Mexican dishes. Used in meats, sauces, chili, sauces and seafood dishes.

Celery seed – Derived from the dried fruit of celery. Used to flavor stews, winter vegetables, egg dishes, fish, pickles, ketchup and tomato juice.

Chervil – An herb similar to parsley that has a more delicate, anise type of flavor.

Chili Powder – Ground cumin, ground chili pepper, ground oregano and powdered garlic. Can also include cloves, salt and/or chocolate. Used in chili con carne, pork and beef dishes, cocktail sauce, steak marinades, cauliflower, corn and Spanish rice.

Chives – An mild flavored herb of the onion family. Also found in a garlic variety. Used to flavor potatoes, eggs, cream soups, chicken, fish, seafood and carrots. Usually added at the end of cooking process. Dry version has less flavor than fresh.

Cilantro - Also known as Chinese parsley. Derived from the same plant as coriander but refers to the leaves and not the seeds. Pepper, spicy flavoring. Mainly used in Oriental and Mexican cooking such as soups, stews, curries, vegetables, dips and salsas.

Cinnamon – A spice with fragrant sweet flavoring. Used to flavor many dishes including fruit salads, puddings, nut milks, sweet desserts, yams, squash and oatmeal.

Cloves – A spice made from the dried flower buds of a clove tree. Its flavoring is pungent yet rich. Used for pickling, in desserts, baked ham spiced drinks and marinades.

Cumin – Aromatic seeds with a warm yet bitter flavoring, used in pickles, chili powders and meat dishes.

Coriander seed – A spice with flavoring that resembles a combination of lemon peel and sage. Commonly used in oriental and curried dishes as well as in pickles and meat dishes.

Curry powder – A blend of 10 to 30 Indian spices. Usually contains garlic, cumin coriander, turmeric and ginger. It is used in all Indian curry recipes. Excellent for flavoring meats, poultry, fish and rice with a touch of oriental flavor.

Dill – An aromatic, clean tasting and fragrant spice that is used as the predominate seasoning in pickles. It is also popularly used in dishes such as macaroni, green apple pie, potato salad and sauerkraut.

Fennel – An herb related to the dill family yet has a stronger flavor than dill but less bitter. Excellent in salads and desserts.

Fenugreek – Member of the legume family and available whole or ground. Bitter, maple-like flavoring. Used frequently in vegetarian diets as a food. Mainly used in Indian and curry cuisine and beef casserole, black bean soup, stews, imitation maple and pickling spices.

Filé gumbo – Thyme and dried sassafras leaves. Used as a thickener for stews, soups, gumbo, meat, poultry and fish sauces.

Fines Herbes – Finely chopped tarragon, chives, parsley and chervil. Can also include watercress, marjoram and savory. Added to dishes and cooked mixtures right before serving without removal.

Garlic – Available in white, pink and purple varieties. Very strong in odor and taste. Comes powdered or fresh. Highly used in Mexican, Mediterranean and Italian dishes. Accents lamb, pork and beef.

Ginger – From ginger root and found fresh, dried, powdered, preserved in syrup, crystallized and pickled. A key ingredient in many Oriental dishes. Used fresh, powdered, or in pickled form with steak, meatloaf, chicken, fish and seafood. Also used with ginger-flavored sherry in recipes, cakes, cookies, puddings, and sweet breads.

Herbs de Provence – A Mediterranean blend of rosemary, thyme, savory, oregano, and marjoram. Can also contain basil, fennel seeds or lavender. Used to season tomato dishes, pizza, stews, chicken and pork.

Italian Seasoning – A blend of rosemary, oregano, thyme, marjoram, basil. Can also contain sage or savory. Used in tomato dishes, dips, herbed breads, with chicken and on pizza.

Mace – A delicate and fragrant spice similar to nutmeg. Used to season fish, fish sauces, baked goods chocolate desserts and stewed fruit.

Marjoram – A potent spice that is similar to mint with a sweet-minty flavor. It is used on roasted lamb and fish, in soups, stews, dried bean dishes, spinach, beverages and jellies.

Mint – An herb that has several hundred varieties with the most common being spearmint and peppermint. Used in teas dried and fresh. Used in numerous dishes such as potatoes, cakes, meats and flavorings for drinks.

Mustard – A spice that is found in whole or ground seed, with coloring from white to black. The white is milder in flavor and used to make yellow mustard while the black varieties are stronger and used for sweet, spicy and beer mustards. Used in salad dressings, barbecue sauces, chowders and cocktail sauces.

Nutmeg – A spice derived from the same tree as Mace. Nutty and cinnamon in flavor. Used in beef, veal and chicken dishes, vegetable stews, in sweet and spicy dishes. Also added to desserts, fruit breads, sauces and eggnog.

Oregano – A popular spice used for seasoning tomato dishes. Especially popular for seasoning pizza and Italian specialty dishes. Also used to flavor breads, egg and cheese dishes, artichokes, cabbage, eggplant and squash.

Paprika – A spice made from a sweet, mild pepper native to Spain. Hungarian versions are dramatically hotter. Brilliant red in color and slightly aromatic. Used as a garnish, for seasoning and in salad dressings.

Parsley – Available in two varieties, curly or flat-leaf. The flat-leaf version is richer and spicier in flavor. Both are available fresh or dried. Used in salads, omelettes, soups, sauces and fish dishes. Used in many dishes to bring out the flavor of other herbs.

Peppercorns – A spice derived from peppercorn berries. Very strong in flavor and aroma and commonly recognized as one of the world's oldest known spices. Peppercorns are available whole and ground. The whole variety is best for maximum freshness. Can be used with any type of dish to add zesty flavoring.

Poppy seeds – Rich crunchy and fragrant seeds with nut-like flavoring. Popular topping for breads, cookies and rolls. A delicious accompaniment to buttered noodles.

Rosemary – A sweet, fresh pine-like herb used in soups, stews, on roast beef and in lamb dishes. Great in cream cheese spread, marinades, tofu pies and casseroles.

Saffron – The most expensive spice available. Spicy and aromatic yet slightly bitter in flavor. Commonly used to flavor and color Spanish dishes, especially rice.

Sage – An herb with minty, camphoraceous flavoring. Commonly used to flavor meats, poultry, sausages, stews and salads. Delicious in egg and cheese dishes, beans, gravies and sauces.

Savory – A relative of the mint family with a peppery and spicy flavoring. Available in summer and winter varieties, but can be used interchangeably. Both varieties are available fresh or dried. Used with beef, chicken and lamb dishes, vegetable soups and beans.

Sesame – An herb widely used in Chinese, Japanese and Middle Eastern dishes. Oil derived from the seeds is popular for its high level of polyunsaturates and vitamin E and absence of cholesterol. Also used as a topping for breads and rolls or sprinkled on baked potatoes, tomatoes and salads.

Star Anise (Chinese anise) – an herb derived from the dried star-shaped fruit of native Chinese and Vietnamese evergreens. Bears no relation to traditional anise but actually similar in flavor with a stronger, licorice taste. Available whole or ground. Commonly used in Chinese and Vietnamese dishes.

Tarragon – A spice commonly used in French dishes. Sweet and bitter in flavor with an undertone of tang. Used in combination with vinegar for salads, cooked asparagus and artichokes.

Thyme –A strong, distinctively flavored herb used to season poultry and fish. Great on sliced tomatoes. Try it in biscuits, bread, vegetable casseroles and pies.

Turmeric – A spice that has a delicate ginger-pepper flavoring. Used as a coloring and flavoring in prepared mustard and in meats, dressings and salads.

Vanilla – Derived from the fully developed fruit of an orchid. Available as whole beans or as an extract. Used to flavor numerous dishes such as desserts, drinks and chocolate.

Common Ingredient Substitutions

Ingredient	Amount	Substitution
Allspice	1 teaspoon	1/2 teaspoon cinnamon and 1/2 teaspoon ground cloves
Baking powder	1 teaspoon	1/4 teaspoon baking soda plus 5/8 teaspoon cream of tartar
Bread crumbs, dry	1/3 cup	1 slice of bread
Bread crumbs, soft	3/4 cup	1 slice of bread
Broth, beef or chicken	1 cup	1 bouillon cube dissolved in 1 cup boiling water
Butter	1 cup	7/8 cup oil and 1/2 teaspoon salt or 1 cup margarine
Buttermilk	1 cup	1 cup plain yogurt or 1 cup minus 1 tablespoon sweet milk, plus 1 tablespoon lemon juice or vinegar (allow to stand 5 to 10 minutes)
Chives, finely chopped	2 teaspoons	2 teaspoons finely chopped green onion tops
Cocoa	1/4 cup or 4 tablespoons	1 ounce (square) chocolate – decrease fat in recipe by 1/2 tablespoon
Coconut cream	1 cup	1 cup cream
Coconut milk	1 cup	1 cup milk
Corn syrup	1 cup	1 cup sugar and 1/4 cup liquid (use type of liquid required in recipe) or 1 cup honey
Cracker crumbs	3/4 cup	1 cup bread crumbs
Cream/half & half Cream, heavy	1 cup 1 cup	1 cup evaporated milk 3/4 cup milk plus 1/3 cup butter or margarine (for use in cooking and baking)

Cream, whipped		Chill 13-ounce can evaporated milk for minimum of 12 hours. Add 1 teaspoon lemon juice and whip until stiff.
Cream, whipping	1 cup	2 tablespoons lemon juice, 2 tablespoons sugar and 1 cup evaporated milk.
Cream of tarter	1/2 teaspoon	1-1/2 teaspoons lemon juice or vinegar
Dill plant, fresh or dried	3 heads	1 tablespoon dill seed
Egg, 1 whole	3 tablespoons	2 egg whites or 1 egg white and 2 teaspoons oil
Egg white	1 white (2 tablespoons)	2 teaspoons sifted dry egg white powder plus 2 tablespoons lukewarm water
Egg yolk	1 yolk (1-1/2 tablespoons)	2 tablespoons sifted dry egg yolk powder plus 2 teaspoons water
Extracts	1 teaspoon	1/4 teaspoon oil of similar flavor
Flour, cake	1 cup sifted	1 cup minus 2 tablespoons sifted all-purpose flour
Flour, self-rising	1 cup	1 cup minus 2 teaspoons all-purpose flour, plus 1-1/2 teaspoons baking powder and 1/2 teaspoon salt
Garlic	1 small clove	1/8 teaspoon garlic powder or 1/4 teaspoon instant minced garlic
Gelatin, flavored	3-ounce package	1 tablespoon plain gelatin plus 2 cups fruit juice
Ginger	1/8 teaspoon, (powdered)	1 tablespoon candied ginger rinsed in water to remove sugar, finely cut, or 1 tablespoon fresh ginger, grated
Herbs, fresh	1 tablespoon finely chopped	1 teaspoon dried herbs or 1/2 teaspoon ground herbs
Honey	1 cup	1-1/4 cups sugar plus 1/4 cup liquid (use liquid required in recipe)
Lemon **Maple sugar**	1 teaspoon juice 1/2 cup	1/2 teaspoon vinegar 1 cup maple syrup
Mushrooms	1 pound fresh	3 ounces dried mushrooms

		6-or 8-ounce can
Onion	1 small	1-1/3 teaspoons onion salt or 1 to 2 tablespoons minced onion or 1 teaspoon onion powder
Orange	1 medium	6 to 8 tablespoons juice
Rum	1/4 cup	1 tablespoon rum extract plus 3 tablespoon liquid (use liquid required in recipe)
Shortening, melted	1 cup	1 cup cooking oil (cooking oil should not be substituted if recipe does not call for melted shortening)
Shortening, (used in baking)	1 cup	1 cup minus 2 tablespoons lard or 1-1/8 cups butter or margarine (decrease salt called for in recipe by 1/2 teaspoon)
Sour cream	1 cup	7/8 cup sour milk or buttermilk plus 1/3 cup butter or margarine
Sugar, brown	1 cup firmly packed	1 cup granular sugar or 1 cup granulated sugar plus 1/4 cup molasses
Sugar, confectioners' or powdered	1 cup	3/4 cup granulated sugar
Sugar, white	1 teaspoon	1/2 to 3/4 teaspoon honey or molasses
Tomatoes, fresh	2 cups, chopped	16-ounce can
Tomato sauce	15-ounce can	6-ounce can tomato paste plus 1 cup water
Tomatoes, chopped	16-ounce can	3 fresh medium tomatoes 16-ounce can stewed tomatoes
Vanilla extract	1 teaspoon	1-inch vanilla bean split and simmered in liquid of recipe
Wine	1 cup	13 tablespoons water, 3 tablespoons lemon juice and 1 tablespoon sugar
Yogurt, plain	1 cup	1 cup buttermilk or 1 cup cottage cheese blended until smooth or 1 cup sour cream

Recipe Index

Bed & Breakfast/Country Inn Index

Blair Manor
Stowe, Vermont
www.blairmanor.com
Best Breakfast in New England – 2005
See recipe, page 69

Blair-Moore House
Bed & Breakfast, The
Jonesborough, Tennessee
www.blairmoorehouse.com
Best Breakfast – 2004
Best Breakfast in the USA – 2005
See recipes, pages 66, 83, 85, 87

Breeden Inn, Carriage House
& Garden Cottage Bed & Breakfast
Bennettsville, South Carolina
www.breedeninn.com
Best Breakfast in the Southeast – 2005
See recipes, pages 36, 72, 135

Casa de San Pedro
Bed and Breakfast Inn
Hereford, Arizona
www.bedandbirds.com
Best Breakfast in the Southwest – 2005
See recipes, pages 24, 124, 139

Celebrations Inn, a Festive
Bed & Breakfast
Pomfret Center, Connecticut
www.celebrationsinn.com
Best Breakfast in New England – 2005
See recipes, pages 18, 28, 119, 137

Chalet Suzanne Country
Inn & Restaurant
Lake Wales, Florida
www.chaletsuzanne.com
Best Breakfast in the Southeast – 2005
See recipe, page 134

Colby Hill Inn
Henniker, New Hampshire
www.colbyhillinn.com
With the Best Chef – 2004
See recipe, page 76

Desert Willow Bed & Breakfast
Jemez Springs, New Mexico
www.desertwillowbandb.com
Best Breakfast in the Southwest – 2005
See recipes, pages 22, 131

Dutch Iris Inn Bed and Breakfast, The
Granby, Connecticut
www.dutchirisinn.com
Best Breakfast in New England – 2005
See recipe, page 58

Earle Clarke House
Victoria, British Columbia
www.earleclarkehouse.com
Best Breakfast in Canada – 2005
See recipe, page 26

Evergreen Inn B&B
Spring Lake Heights, New Jersey
www.evergreeninn.net
Best Breakfast in the Northeast – 2005
See recipes, pages 31, 64, 81

Forgett-Me-Nott Bed & Breakfast
Victoria, British Columbia
www3.telus.net/forgettmenott
Best Breakfast in Canada – 2005
See recipes, pages 38, 60, 90

Henry Whipple House Bed & Breakfast
Bristol, New Hampshire
www.thewhipplehouse.com
Best Breakfast in New England – 2005
See recipes, pages 39, 78

Historic Inns of Abingdon:
Victoria & Albert Inn and
Love House Bed & Breakfast
Abingdon, Virginia
www.abingdon-virginia.com
Best Breakfast – 2004
See recipes, pages 75, 110, 118

Homeridge Bed and Breakfast, The
Jerseyville, Illinois
www.homeridge.com
Best Breakfast in the USA – 2005
See recipe, page 62

Hughes Hacienda Bed & Breakfast
Colorado Springs, Colorado
www.hugheshacienda.com
Best Breakfast in the Southwest – 2005
See recipes, pages 19, 34, 44, 122

Inn at the Bay Bed & Breakfast
St. Petersburg, Florida
www.innatthebay.com
Best Breakfast in the Southeast – 2005
See recipe, page 57

Inn Britannia
Searsport, Maine
www.innbritannia.com
Best Breakfast in New England – 2005
See recipes, pages 17, 142

**John F. Craig House
Bed & Breakfast, The**
Cape May, New Jersey
www.johnfcraig.com
Best Breakfast in the Northeast – 2005
See recipes, pages 42, 70, 82, 93, 126,
132, 136, 144, 149

Katherine's Bed and Breakfast
Asheville, North Carolina
www.katherinesbandb.com
Best Breakfast in the Southeast – 2005
See recipe, page 37

Kensington Riverside Inn (On the Cover)
Calgary, Alberta
www.kensingtonriversideinn.com
For the Most Perfect Stay - 2005
See recipe, page15

Lococo House II Bed & Breakfast
St. Charles, Missouri
www.lococohouse.com
Best Breakfast – 2004
See recipe, page 67

Mill Creek Homestead Bed & Breakfast
Bird-in-Hand, Pennsylvania
www.millcreekhomestead.com
Best Breakfast in the Northeast – 2005
See recipes, pages 55, 109, 145

Morning Glory Inn
Slatyfork, West Virginia
www.morninggloryinn.com
Best Breakfast – 2004
Best Breakfast in the Northeast – 2005
See recipe, page 52

Painted Lady Bed and Breakfast, The
Elmira, New York
www.thepaintedlady.net
Best Breakfast in the Northeast – 2005
See recipes, pages 33, 40, 104, 130

Pikes Peak Paradise Bed and Breakfast
Woodland Park, Colorado
www.pikespeakmall.com/pppbandb
Best Breakfast in the Southwest – 2005
See recipes, pages 21, 59

**Reagan's Queen Anne
Bed and Breakfast**
Hannibal, Missouri
www.reagansqueenanne.com
Best Breakfast in the USA – 2005
See recipes, pages 46, 63

Roaring Lion Bed and Breakfast, The
Waldoboro, Maine
www.roaringlion.com
Best Breakfast in New England – 2005
See recipes, pages 68, 88

Roosevelt, a Bed and Breakfast Inn, The
Coeur d'Alene, Idaho
www.therooseveltinn.com
Best Breakfast in the Northwest – 2005
See recipe, page 32

Wander Inn
Newport, Rhode Island
www.wanderinn.com
With the Best Chef – 2004
See recipes, pages 30, 56, 138, 154

Wyman Hotel & Inn, The
Silverton, Colorado
www.thewyman.com
With the Best Chef – 2004
See recipes, pages 20, 98, 102, 103, 116, 133

Bibliography

ACH Food Companies, Inc. "Spice Advice®." 2005. <www.spiceadvice.com>.

American Egg Board. "Basic Egg Facts & FAQ's." 2005. <www.aeb.org>.

Castello Cities Internet Network. "Banana.Com." 2005. <www.banana.com>.

E-Cookbooks.net - The Food & Cooking Network. "Ingredient Substitutions." 2005. <www.e-cookbooks.net/ingresub.htm>.

Ehler, James T. "Food Reference Website." 2005. <www.foodreference.com>.

eNotes.com LLC. "William Shakespeare at eNotes." 2005. <www.allshakespeare.com>.

Floridata.com, LC. "Flori-Data™." 2005. <www.floridata.com>.

InDepthInfo.com. "In Depth Info.Com." 2005. <www.indepthinfo.com>.

Jaworski, Stephanie. "Scone Newsletter." 2005. <www.joyofbaking.com>.

Matthews, Bob. "Pumpkin Nook."2005. <www.pumpkinnook.com>.

Olver, Lynne. "Food Timeline-Culinary History Timeline." 2005. <www.foodtimeline.org>.

Stradley, Linda. "What's Cooking America." 2005. <www.whatscookingamerica.net>.

The Home of Food Network. "Food Network.Com." 2005. <www.foodtv.com>.

Weber® Stephen Products. "Spice & Herb Chart" 2005. <www.weber.com/bba/pub/recipe/grilling101/spiceherb.aspx>.

Wild Blueberry Association of North America. "The Power of Blue™." 2005. <www.wildblueberries.com>.

Notes . . .

Notes . . .

Notes . . .

Notes . . .

Notes . . .